KIDS ON THE MOVE

Creative Movement
For Children of All Ages

Kassandra Schmutz Boyd
Melanie Schmutz Chalk
Jennifer Schmutz Law

Lightning Source

Kids on the Move: Creative Movement for Children of All Ages ©

Copyright © 2003 by Creative Publishing

Published by:
Creative Publishing
2221 Justin Road #119-123
Flower Mound, Texas 75028
www.creativekidsonthemove.com

Send all requests for information to the above address.

Printed in the United States of America

What is Creative Movement?

Creative Movement is a joyful way to explore movement through music, develop physical skills, channel energy, stimulate imagination and promote creativity. It provides children with opportunities for noncompetitive, success-oriented and creative experiences. This program includes creative moving taught through rhyme, games, musical story telling, instrument playing, props, and development of basic concepts like rhythm, directionality, perception, and memory.

Table of Contents

About the Authors

Kassandra S. Boyd

Kassandra began dancing at the age of 4 and has danced ever since. She earned her Bachelors Degree in Dance from the University of Houston, and has taught jazz, tap, ballet, clogging, gymnastics and creative movement for 16 years. She choreographed and performed in several shows at Six Flags Amusement Park. She has judged beauty pageants and cheerleading competitions, as well as choreographing for drill teams. Kassie danced her way to placing third runner-up in a preliminary to the Miss America Pageant. As Dance Director, Kassie instigated dance programs at various recreation centers in Oklahoma, Houston and Dallas. She continues to perform in local area plays and musicals. Her hobbies include working as a certified personal trainer, cake decorating, and candle making. Kassie resides in Dallas with her husband Michael, and three children, Sterling (7), Savannah (4) and Stefan (2).

Melanie S. Chalk

Melanie received her Bachelors Degree from Rice University, double majoring in Vocal Music and Sociology. She earned her Masters Degree in Communication from The University of Houston. Melanie has taught voice and piano lessons for 15 years, and has implemented creative movement programs in various Houston-area daycare centers and schools. Melanie performed for several years as a singer/dancer at Six Flags Amusement Park, and toured Africa as a member of the Brigham Young University Young Ambassadors. Melanie is a National Anthem soloist for various teams, including the Houston Astros and Utah Jazz. She currently enjoys composing music, traveling, calligraphy, and gardening. She lives in Houston, Texas, with her husband, Daron, and their two children, Stephen (3) and Kassandra (1).

Jennifer S. Law

Jennifer has been innovating unique child-play activities for years. She sharpened her creative skills as the Owner/Coordinator for numerous craft show exhibitions in Texas. Jenny earned her Associates Degree in Liberal Arts from Tulsa Junior College. She has served as the President of the Young Womens Organization at her church, enjoying directing road shows and choreographing skits. She studied dance for several years in Oklahoma, where she also performed in community productions. Jenny currently teaches creative movement in the Dallas/Ft.Worth area. She is taking karate with her son, and is working toward her black belt. She lives with her husband Gordon, and their four children: Jessica (13), Desiree (11), Cannon (9), and Beaumont (4).

Introduction

Children love to move! In fact, they are rarely still. Children experience great joy simply by moving freely to different rhythms. By implementing this Creative Movement Program, you are offering endless opportunities for children to further develop their love of movement, music and creativity.

Music and movement are in every child. As teachers, we must let it out! This program is designed to help your children physically, musically, socially, and mentally. *Kids on the Move©* will assist you in planning different movement classes which will enhance children's education in the following ways:

≋ *BODY AWARENESS* improves. Children gain a better mental picture of their own body. Controlling their bodies is the initial type of control children have over themselves. It is the first step toward developing internal control and self-discipline.

≋ *SELF CONTROL, FOCUS AND ABILITY TO CONCENTRATE* are enhanced. Creative movement requires some degree of concentration. Once children understand what 'focusing' feels like, they are better able to concentrate in other areas of life.

≋ *RESPECT* increases as children become aware of others with whom they come in contact. Children learn and accept the fact that all bodies come in various sizes and shapes. They also learn to respect these differences in their peers.

≋ *CONTRIBUTIONS IN THE CLASSROOM* become more frequent and productive. Creative movement channels energy, which enables children to release tension, and get the wiggles out.

≋ *COGNITIVE LEARNING* is stimulated by dancing. Moving and sensory consciousness are the main ways children learn about their world and themselves. Learning is facilitated when a child's entire body is involved.

≋ *SELF-ESTEEM* is possibly the greatest benefit from incorporating creative movement into any curriculum. As children develop new skills, their sense of worth and confidence will increase.

Remember:

1. Observation is participation! Children will participate when they are ready. Always try to create a positive learning environment, and don't force the child to participate.
2. Be sure to give plenty of positive reinforcement throughout the class (See Appendix 5).
3. Focus on what children CAN do, rather than what they CAN'T do.
4. It is important to feel children's participation level. If they act bored and disinterested, quickly move on to a different activity.

5. Keep teacher-directed activities to a minimum so that children's imagination can develop.
6. Utilize a wide variety of music with an assortment of speeds and rhythms.
7. Read the lesson in advance to be fully prepared and to enhance learning.
8. Have patience. LEARNING new skills can be difficult, but KNOWING these skills brings great joy!
9. Never compare one child to another. Every child is an individual and develops at his/her own speed.
10. Share curiosities with children. Ask them questions and be interested in what they are doing.
11. Don't be too eager to help children. It is amazing to see how creative and imaginative children can be without help from the instructor.
12. Make each class cheerful and fun. Be positive about children's successes and sympathetic about their failures.
13. Create an appropriate teaching atmosphere where children are free to take risks.

Advantages This Book Offers:

1. Each lesson contains curriculum outlined with easy-to-follow instructions.
2. Anyone can teach the classes; no degree, specific training, or music is required.
3. Creative movement is not limited to specific ages or gender.
4. Special needs children (those with sensory, communication, developmental or physical challenges) can also participate. For example, children in wheelchairs can participate by attaching props in different ways to their bodies or wheelchairs. They can also keep the beat by blinking or nodding their heads. All children love and benefit from music.

Suggestions For Use:

1. Classroom should be ready for each class prior to beginning the lesson. Carpet squares or matching shirts work well because they give children a visual cue that creative movement is about to begin.
2. Instructors should hold classes one or two days per week. Children begin to look forward to class as a 'special time.'
3. Monthly handouts can be developed based on the class outlines; these give parents and caregivers valuable feedback regarding the curriculum being studied (See App. 6).
4. Teach one lesson twice in one week. Repetition assists in the learning process.
5. Teach two different lessons in one week; repeat the same two lessons the following week.
6. Teach separate lessons by mixing and matching. This allows for greater variety.
7. Find lessons that incorporate what is being taught in the classroom for that particular week for congruency.

We hope you have as much fun using this book as we had in writing it! We have tried to implement different aspects of movement in each lesson plan. We have included a glossary for technical terms and photographs for a better understanding of positions. It is our hope that you enjoy the numerous benefits which come from creative movement!

Lesson Outlines

Lesson #1: Animal Day

Objectives: To practice running, jumping, hopping, spinning, and balancing. To develop skills in directionality, spatial relations, cooperation, and moving through general space safely. To practice animal actions and locomotor movements.

Materials Needed: Stuffed animals (1 per child; ask children in advance to bring their own) Towel (1 per pair)

Class Outline:

A.   Warm-ups* (See App. 1)
B.   Activities
    1. *Animal Play.* Children scatter stuffed animals around room. Start music. Children do following: run and jump *over*, not *on* the animals, hold and love animals, cradle and rock animals, toss and catch animals.
    2. *Team Tossing.* Pair children. Give each team a towel and an animal. Use towel to bounce animal up and down, and swing it back and forth.
    3. *Let's Pretend.* Children lay down with heads on floor. Chant: "sleeping, sleeping, all the children are sleeping. When they wake up, they are a dog!" Children get up and pretend to be dogs. Repeat, changing the animal. Children switch between pretending to be the animal and resting.
    4. *Animal Shapes.* Children spread out around room. Call out an animal and children make their bodies into the *shape* of that animal. For example, a frog: squat down low and puff out cheeks. Repeat with: cat, snake, cow, giraffe, monkey, elephant, bunny, lion, horse, fish, octopus, spider, duck, bee, worm, bird, ant, squirrel, caterpillar, butterfly, kitten, elephant, horse, cow, kangaroo, ape, whale, seal, bear, hippopotamus, turtle, snail, flamingo, fox, dog, and horse.
    5. *Animal Action Game.* Sit in circle with one child in center. That child chooses an animal to act out. Continue until someone correctly guesses animal. Repeat until each child has a turn.
    6. *Dog, Dog, Cat!* Play "Duck, Duck, Goose" but use different animals instead. For example: one child moves around circle saying, "dog, dog, dog, cat!" while gently touching a child on head. The child who is touched chases first child around circle. Repeat. Modification: switch animals each time; instead of running around circle, children must imitate the animal.
    7. *Hula Hoop Game.* Children pretend to be a lion and jump through a 'ring of fire' while roaring. Hold hula hoop horizontally over children while they move back and forth traveling under hoop. They can put their animal on their back, and take it for a ride while traveling under hoop.
    8. *Old MacDonald Had a Farm.* Children simultaneously become a different animal. Teacher says, "Freeze!" and one by one, touches children on head. Children dance back to their place on the farm and 'go to sleep.'

Lesson #2: Beanbag Day

Objectives: To develop coordination, balance, body part identification, and rhythm. To provide aerobic activity and to strengthen the cardiovascular system.

Materials Needed: Beanbags (1 per child)
                           Masking tape
                           Boogie-woogie type music

Class Outline:

A.   Warm-ups* (See App. 1)
B.   Activities

1. _Beanbag Toss & Catch_. Children stand up straight and gently toss beanbag in air. Now toss and catch beanbag with a friend.
2. _Beanbag Circle Toss_. Children form a circle. One child tosses a beanbag to next child. Then, one child calls out a name and tosses beanbag to them. The child who catches it calls someone else's name and tosses beanbag to them. Continue.
3. _Beanbag Kick_. Place beanbag on the floor and _gently_ kick it around the room, alternating feet. Pair children. Kick beanbag back and forth to each other several times with each foot.
4. _Beanbag Carry_. Create a path on floor with masking tape: straight, circular, zig-zag, or wavy. Children follow path while balancing beanbag on different body parts: head, shoulder, toe, back, knee, elbow, hand, forehead, finger, ear, tummy, arm, nose, wrist, foot, leg and chest. Place beanbag under chin, under arm and between knees. Explore ways of moving while balancing beanbag on body parts.
5. _Happy Sunshine_. Several children lay on floor forming a large circle with bodies. Remaining children lay out, flat and straight from circle, as the 'sunshine beams.' Say the following while children do actions: "the sunshine is getting hotter and hotter" (children shake bodies); the sunshine is feeling silly (wiggle bodies while laughing); the sunshine is going to bed" (group rolls into large moon shape on floor); sunshine is awake again (scurry into sunshine position again).
6. _Beanbag Boogie_. Play boogie music while children dance with beanbags. Have them move different ways: jumping, stomping, shaking, twisting and rocking.
7. _Beanbag Freeze_. Start and stop music at various intervals. When music stops, call out a body part to put beanbag on. Children dance to music with beanbags while music plays. While freezing, children keep body perfectly still. Repeat.
8. _Beanbag March_. Children march around room with beanbag on one body part. Others follow line-leader. Children take turns leading, then go to end of line. Continue marching with knees lifted high until everyone has had a turn leading.
9. _Beanbag Pass_. Children stand in circle and pass beanbag to person beside them in following ways: over head, under an arm, under one lifted leg, balancing on a body part (elbow, shoulder, finger, etc.).
10. _Bean Bag Line_. Line up beanbags in a line with spaces between them. Children hop over each beanbag with two feet, then with one foot. Weave in and out of the beanbags. Tip-toe on top of each beanbag.

Lesson #3: Blanket Day

Objectives: To explore various relaxation techniques. To practice concentration, body control, flexibility, and balance.

Materials Needed: Small blankets (1 per child; ask children in advance to bring their own)
A sheet

Class Outline:

A. Warm-ups* (See App. 1)
B. Activities
   1. *Blanket Roll.* Children roll blankets like a tube and lay them horizontally on ground in front of them. Keeping feet in same place, bend over and touch blanket with both hands. Then slowly unroll blanket. Push blanket forward until child is lying on stomach. Stretch arms as far forward as possible, legs as far behind as possible. Teacher says, "Great stretch!"
   2. *I'm Stuck!* Children lay blanket flat on floor and stand in the middle of it. Say, "You're stuck on your blanket, and you can't move off. What kind of movements can you do in such a small place?"
   3. *Fast Asleep.* Children fold blanket into a pillow shape. Say, "Your head is fast asleep." Children put their head on their 'pillow.' Continue by naming different body parts and putting them on their pillows. End with their head on pillow.
   4. *Grab It.* Begin with blanket smooth on floor. Children stand with toes next to blanket. Grab blanket tightly with toes, curling it tightly under toes. Walk backward to make blanket slide along floor. Ideas for blanket movement: kick, stand, sit, and lay on floor on back and stomach. Move legs behind you while laying on floor. Kick to side; pass blanket to neighbor with toes; lay on back and kick in air while holding blanket with toes; drop and catch the blanket on face. Wrinkle blanket to make it as small possible, then smooth blanket out again and wrinkle with different parts: elbow, knee, bottom, head, etc.
   5. *Blanket Balance.* Roll up sheet so it looks like a tube. Walk on blanket from one end to the other like a tight-rope walker. Balance while walking backward and sideways.
   6. *Tug of War.* Divide children and use rolled sheet to play tug of war.
   7. *Jump Rope Blanket.* Children roll blankets like a tube. Hold each end with hands. Lower arms and step over blanket, holding it tightly. Step first with one foot and then the other. Now go backward. Repeat. Next, children lay tube-shaped blanket on floor and run and jump over it. Next jump side to side over it.
   8. *Floating Blanket.* Children stretch out their whole body on their blanket, lying on their stomach. Explain that they should rest quietly on their blanket until it is their turn. Turn on soft lullaby music. Grasp one end of a blanket, and walk backward, pulling the blanket with the child on top of it. When finished, move on to the next child. Repeat until every child has had a turn.
   9. *Turtle, Turtle.* Children hide underneath blanket in turtle position. With blanket as 'shell,' poke head then other body parts out of shell.

Lesson #4: Body Day

Objectives: To increase body perception through mirroring, isolation, and naming of body parts. To develop personal and general space concepts while problem-solving and multi-tasking.

Materials Needed: Large-sized bubble wrap (one 12" x 12" sheet per child)
Paper plates (1 per child)
Music with varying rhythms
Action Cards* (See App. 4)
Balls (1 per child)

Class Outline:

A.   Warm-ups* (See App. 1)
B.   Activities
    1. *Bubble Wrap.* Children place bubble wrap on floor in front of them. Pop bubbles WITHOUT using hands. As music plays, pop bubbles using elbows, knees, toes, and bottoms. Stomp bubbles with shoes on and with bare feet.
    2. *Paper Plate Dancing.* Children keep the beat by tapping plate on head, tummy, foot, knee, arm, etc.
    3. *My Body.* Teacher names two body parts and children must determine the best way to move both parts simultaneously: lift two of the same parts (two arms, two legs), lift two different parts (foot and arm, elbow and knee), hide body parts (hands behind back, feet under bottom), move body parts different ways (wave hand, shake foot, tap finger, rub head, pat hips, wiggle toe, etc.)
    4. *What Can Body Parts Do?* Prepare Action Cards. One by one, children select an Action Card and class performs that action.
    5. *Be My Mirror.* Two children stand facing each other. While facing (mirroring) each other, take turns choosing a movement and copying it.
    6. *Be My Shadow.* One child stands behind another child, both facing same direction. Child behind imitates movements of child in front. Change positions and repeat.
    7. *Body Part Roll.* Children begin with ball on head. As music plays, roll it to another part of body making no sound. Move quietly, softly, slowly and smoothly. Roll it around legs, arms, neck, and face. Sit on floor and roll it around feet. Lie on floor. Where else can they roll it... on back, or on stomach?
    8. *Rhythm Train.* Children line up behind teacher, holding waist of child in front of them. Move around room like a train, trying different rhythms.
    9. *Look What My Body Can Do.* Teacher asks children to perform following tasks: nuzzle noses with a friend, tickle friend's toes, wiggle chin with fingers, attach ear to friend's ear, use arms to hug a friend, and gently pinch own cheeks. Then ask children what other things they can do with their bodies.
    10. *Characterize.* Children pretend they are opening birthday presents as the following: a 2-year old child, 10-year old child, a very old grandparent, mom, dad.
    11. *Creative Time.* As music plays, children dance any way they desire.

Lesson #5: Bug Day

Objectives: To promote quick thinking and sharing of ideas while increasing awareness, memory, and listening skills.

Materials Needed: White strings (cut in 6' strips; 1 per pair)
Cotton balls
A bucket
Plastic flowers
Busy 'bumblebee' music (i.e.: 'Flight of the Bumblebee')
A ball

Class Outline:

A. Warm-ups* (See App. 1)
B. Activities
1. *Be a Bug*. Discuss different bugs; children become the following:
   - cricket: sit with one leg extended. Cross calves and rub them together.
   - firefly: walk around hunched over with wrists touching on bottoms. Flash (open/shut) fingers.
   - praying mantis: crouch down, with both hands making claws; one arms extends beyond the other.
   - mosquito: use arm to pretend to have a long sucking nose.
   - other suggestions: slug, butterfly, ladybug, ant, potato bug.
2. *Centipede** (See App. 2). Children get on hands and knees facing same direction. Each child holds ankles of child in front of them. Simultaneously, everyone crawls in same direction.
3. *Ant, Ant, Fly*. Play "Duck, Duck, Goose" but use bugs instead. For example: one child moves around circle saying, "ant, ant, ant, fly!" while gently touching a child on head. The child who is touched chases first child around circle. Repeat.
4. *Spider Dance*. Pair children. As music plays, each child holds one end of a string. They pretend to be a spider while spinning a web, weaving in and out.
5. *Worker Ants*. Spread cotton balls all over floor. Teacher is the Queen Ant and sits in center of room. Children march around, searching for 'food' (cotton balls). After gathering the food, they march back to the ant hill and feed the Queen Ant, who is holding a bucket for the food.
6. *Caterpillar*. Children lie on their stomach, body extended. Ask, "If you are a caterpillar, can you walk without bending your arms and legs?" Pretend you've climbed up onto a leaf to have a nap. Show how still and sleepy a caterpillar would be. Look for quiet, easy breathing. Change to a butterfly. Wiggle on floor from side to side with bottoms in air. Walk forward with hands, then forward with feet to meet hands 'inch-worm' style. Roll across floor and curl into a cocoon. Be very still, then break from cocoon, stretch wings, and flutter like a butterfly.
7. *Musical Beehives*. Play busy music. Spread plastic flowers around room. Children pretend they are bees and fly from flower to flower.

Lesson #6: Career Day

Objectives: To gain an understanding of the people who serve in the community. To explore sequencing and level changes, and to use imaginations.

Materials Needed: Hats (or pictures of hats)
Paint brush (1 per child)
Aprons (1 per child)
Two boxes
Envelopes (1 per child)
Red circle stickers
'Stop & Go' Sign (sign with **_STOP_** on one side and **_GO_** on other)
Bucket of plastic tools (1 per child)
Beanbags (1 per child)

Class Outline:

A.   Warm-ups* (See App. 1)
B.   Activities.
   1. _Hats_. Experience different careers by putting on different hats!
      - _Baker:_ With apron, role play different cooking actions: stirring, chopping, rolling.
      - _Farmer:_ Role play different farm actions: feed animals, milk cows, dig in garden, plant seeds.
      - _Artist:_ When music begins, 'paint' wall with paintbrush. Call out different levels for them to work at: high, low, middle.
      - _Mail Carrier:_ Place a box at each end of room, one empty, and the other filled with envelopes. Children form a line by the box with envelopes. When music begins, children take turns picking up an envelope and carrying it to the empty box. Children perform different locomotor movements each time they cross the room* (See App. 4).
      - _Clown:_ Put a red circle sticker on each child's nose. Demonstrate different ways to walk, and encourage them to create their own 'silly' walk.
      - _Police Officer:_ Play 'Red Light Green Light.' Children line up at one end of room and Teacher stands at other, turning sign back and forth.
      - _Sailor:_ Children sit on floor, legs apart, facing partner. With feet touching, hold hands. One leans back and pulls while the other pushes forward. Then switch, producing a rowing motion.
      - _Construction Worker:_ Each child chooses one tool from a bucket. When music begins, make movement relative to tool. When music stops, children run back to bucket and switch tools.
      - _Additional Ideas:_ firefighter, train engineer, taxi driver, welder, paramedic.
   2. _The Hat Parade!_ Children wear hats while marching in a line. Teacher calls their name, and they respond by saying what type of helper they are imitating.
   3. _Hat Pass._ Stand in circle with hats on head. Take hats off, turn around with hat pulled into tummy, touch hat to floor, pass it to person beside them. Continue.
   4. _Hat Toss._ Toss beanbags into own hat. Pick up and repeat.

Lesson #7: Circus Day

Objectives: To develop listening skills, creativity, and balance through pantomime.

Materials Needed: Clown hats or bows (1 per child)
Beanbags or balls (1 per child)
Large scarves (1 per child)
1 Hula Hoop
Rope or masking tape
Musical instruments (1 per child; i.e.: kazoos, maracas, drums, cymbals)

Class Outline:

A. Warm-ups* (See App. 1)
B. Activities
1. _Ringmaster_. Teacher says: "Ladies, gentlemen, and children of all ages, the circus parade is about to begin!"
2. _Be A Clown_. 'Clowns' (children) enter circle skipping happily, doing cartwheels and waving. Exaggerate smiles and frowns with hand and facial gestures. Walk in different, creative and silly ways: backward, holding ankles, tall, squatty, pretending to trip. Juggle with balls or beanbags.
3. _Prancing Ponies_. 'Ponies' (children) enter circle galloping. Get into straight line, make prancing motions, lift knees up high, and kick up rear feet. Put one foot forward and count to ten by tapping toes as if pawing ground.
4. _Flying Trapeze_.* (See App. 2) 'Trapeze artists' (children) strut into circle wearing 'capes' (scarves). Pantomime a climbing motion as they climb the ladder to platform. Fly through air on a trapeze by standing hunched over, scooping arms from down below and raising them up to sky while going up on tip toes with arms extended overhead. Reverse, going backward. Perform 'spins' in air. Climb down and strut away.
5. _Animal Acts_. Children pantomime the following:
    - _Bears:_ Enter circle doing bear walk: get on all fours and simultaneously lift right arm and leg, then left arm and leg.
    - _Elephants*_ (See App. 2): Clasp hands together so arms look like trunks. Do beginning of a headstand, balancing knees on elbows. Bend forward holding right arm in front like a trunk. Put left hand through legs, reach behind, and grab the "trunk" (right hand) of elephant behind them; now walk.
    - _Lions:_ Enter on all fours. Teacher holds a hula hoop; children jump through, roar, shake manes, line up in a row, roll onto sides, then sit up.
    - _Seals:_ Enter walking on hands, dragging legs behind. Balance a ball on nose, then toss to each other. Lean back and clap hands together.
6. _Tightrope Walker_. Children enter circle wearing scarf around waist. Pantomime climbing a ladder to tightrope. Place a rope or strip of masking tape across floor for tightrope. Children walk across forward and backward.
7. _Marching Band_. Give each child a different instrument for the circus finale!

Lesson #8: Color Day

Objectives: To enhance memory, listening skills and color recognition.

Materials Needed: Many large colored feathers
An orange
Spoons (1 per child)
Four differently colored cones
Large ball
Music with varied rhythm and tempo
Large sheets of butcher paper
Crayons (1 per child)
Bucket of differently colored strips of material (1 per child)

Class Outline:

A. Warm-ups* (See App. 1)
B. Activities
   1. _Feather Dancing._ Give each child a colored feather to dance with. While music plays, keep feather in air by blowing it. Next, throw entire bag of feathers in air while children gather their own little bunches. For clean up, assign each child a color to pick up and bring back to bag.
   2. _Orange Pass._ Children sit in a large circle, each holding a spoon. Pass orange from one child to next using spoons. If the orange falls, pick it up, put it back on spoon and continue passing. Then, pass orange to each other under chins without using hands.
   3. _Move the Ball._ Put four cones in four corners of room. Gather children in middle of room with a ball. Children must decide how they will get ball from middle of room to correctly colored cone. Choose a way that involves the cooperation of everyone: roll, kick, carry, throw, pass, etc. Call out a color and they begin. Praise them when they reach the cone! Repeat process, using each movement only once.
   4. _Draw the Music._ Cover a table with butcher paper. Children walk around table with crayon in hand, making movements on paper to beat of the music. Play a stop and go 'freeze' game to varied music; this activity combines art, music and movement. Children should draw what the music sounds like!
   5. _Color Dancing._ Place a bucket of material strips in middle of room. Play different types of music and ask children how the music makes them feel. Let them choose their own color and dance with it. Allow them to change colors as music changes. Children move material to beat of the music. Talk about the music; is it fast, slow, happy, or sad? All the colors flowing through the air will brighten any class!
   6. _Color Memory._ Demonstrate specific movements that correspond with each colored cone. Review actions with children. Then hold up cones as children perform actions without teacher prompting: red - bang on floor; purple - skitter across floor; orange - spin in place; blue - clap.

Lesson #9: Cowboy Day

Objectives: To develop cooperation, coordination, body control, tactile senses, fine motor skills, and imagination.

Materials Needed: Cowboy hats (Ask children in advance to bring their own)
Stick horses (or dowel rods; 1 per child)
Hula hoops
A bouncing horse (or upside-down bucket)
One 5-ft pliable cotton rope (1 per child)
Sheriff's badges and vests* (See App. 3)
Rubber snake
Band-aids (1 per child)
Red and white checked table cloth
Bucket of plastic food (from a play kitchen)
Two bowls, one empty and one with beans
3 oz. cups (1 per child)
Two boxes, one empty and one with envelopes

Class Outline:
A. Warm-ups* (See App. 1)
B. Activities
    1. *Ridin' A Horse.* Give each child a stick horse and have them 'ride' around room.
    2. *Lasso That Horse.* Set up a 'bouncing' horse in middle of room. Give each child a hula hoop to 'lasso' their horse. Then have them jump through their hoop.
    3. *Sheriff.* Create an imaginary street with masking tape. Children put on badges and vests, hook thumbs in pants and travel down street using different locomotor movements* (See App. 4).
    5. *My Lasso.* Teacher holds one end of rope. Children pretend rope is a snake. Slowly shake rope along floor imitating the slithering of a snake. Gradually get faster; children follow snake and jump over it.
    6. *Rattlesnake.* Pass the rattlesnake while music plays. Whoever is holding it when music stops gets bitten and receives a band aid. Play until everyone has a band-aid! Next, children hold edges of table cloth while tossing and catching snake.
    7. *Chuck Wagon.* Children sit in circle around bucket of plastic food. Each child chooses one food item. As Teacher says, "pass," each child passes item to right and receives item from left. Continue.
    8. *Pass the Beans.* Place bowls at each end of room. Children form line between bowls, each holding a cup. Child closest to bowl of beans scoops beans then dumps them into their neighbor's cup. Continue passing. The child at end of row dumps beans into empty bowl. Continue until all beans have been moved from one bowl to the other.
    9. *Pony Express.* Place box at each end of room, one empty and other filled with envelopes. Children form a line by the envelopes. When music begins, children take turns picking up an envelope and galloping to empty box.

Lesson #10: Dance Day

Objectives: To demonstrate rhythmic accuracy and repetition while experiencing basic movement concepts. To encourage following directions, moving in unison, and spatial awareness through cardiovascular activities.

Materials Needed: Paper plates (1 per child)
Scarves (1 per child)
Hawaiian music
Hula skirts and shakers* (See App. 3)

Class Outline:

A.   Warm-ups* (See App. 1)
B.   Activities
  1. _Naming a Dance._ The naming of a dance involves a child's association between a movement and a word. As imagination takes them through various stages of exploration, a name is given to a short movement sequence. The sequence is repeated into a pattern and it becomes a dance. Encourage children to interpret the following images:
      - _Kite dance._ Sequences of rising, floating, twisting and falling.
      - _Robot dance._ Sequences of mechanical, angular movements.
      - _Puppet dance._ Sequences of bouncing, pulling, swinging and jiggling.
      - _Bird dance._ Sequences of flying, perching, and pecking.
      - _Mouse dance._ Sequences of creeping, sneaking and pouncing.
  2. _Paper Plate Dancing._ Give each child a plate. Play different types of music while children keep the beat with different tapping movements. Tap plate on different body parts: head, tummy, foot, knee. Give children a second plate; put plates on floor. Stand on plates and pretend to ice-skate.
  3. _Scarf Dancing._ Give each child a scarf. Children move scarves to beat of music. Dip and twirl scarf gracefully. Talk about the music. Is it fast, slow, happy, sad?
  4. _Hula Dance._ Wearing hula skirts, children dance to Hawaiian music as they move their arms and hips in a hula fashion.
  5. _Dance With Me._ As the leader, one child stands in the middle of circle and leads a dance. Change leaders and repeat.
  6. _Toilet Paper Dance._ Bring several rolls of toilet paper. Children hold toilet paper in hands and dance around teacher, wrapping the paper around the teacher. Wrap other things or toss and catch while dancing. Children will enjoy cleaning up too!
  7. _Create a Dance._ Give children three minutes to 'create' their own dance. They can use any prop available. One by one, children perform dance for class.
  8. _Shaker Dance._ Use shakers and dance around room* (see App. 3).
  9. _Mousetrap._ Divide children; half are the 'trap' (sit in circle holding hands), while half are the 'mice' (skip around circle). Mice dance in and out of circle; when music stops, trap snaps shut, capturing mice. Mice that are caught inside join the circle. Continue.

Lesson #11: Dinosaur Day

Objectives: To visualize the dinosaur era through pantomime, full body stretching, and imagination.

Materials Needed: Pictures depicting dinosaurs and their environment
A collection of toy dinosaurs
Long light-weight scarves (1 per child)

Class Outline:

A. Warm-ups* (See App. 1)
B. Activities
 1. _Greeting_. Greet children with a growl! Have a roaring contest. Then show pictures of diverse types of dinosaurs. Emphasize their distinctive shapes and methods of moving and obtaining food.
 2. _Dino Actions_. Children spread out and re-create the following actions of dinosaurs: eat high or low plants, with a long neck nibble leaves from the treetops, wallow through a shallow swamp, hide from a rival, creep up and pounce on a rival, run in fear, rest in the sun, waddle like a duck, walk like you weigh as much as 12 elephants and you are as long as several school buses, roar and show teeth and claws, lay eggs, feed your young. Once movements are established, assign each child a different dinosaur movement. Create a scene by having children perform the different actions simultaneously.
 3. _Fly Pterranodon_. Give each child a scarf to use as wings. Have them hold two corners of scarf in each extended hand, with scarf behind them. Teacher says, "fly" and encourage children to stretch their arms way out and up.
 4. _Dino Jump_. Children scatter toy dinosaurs around room. When music starts, they run and jump _over_ them, not _on_ them. Then children get on hands and knees to push or scoot dinos on the floor with nose.
 5. _Dino Dance_. Children stomp around like dinosaurs doing a friendly dino dance.
 6. _Dino Walking_* (See App. 2). Pair children. One child stands immediately behind the other and wraps arms around waist of child in front. Practice walking like a dinosaur. Take big, giant steps together, stepping with their right feet, then with left feet. Child in rear can hold scarf for tail. Remind them that they are huge, two-ton dinosaurs, slowly walking on giant feet!
 7. _T-Rex, T-Rex, Brontosaurus!_ Play "Duck, Duck, Goose" but use dinosaurs instead. For example, one child moves around circle saying, "T-Rex, T-Rex, Brontosaurus!" while gently touching a child on head. The child who is touched chases first child around circle. Repeat with other dinosaurs: Iguanodon, Stegosaurus, Raptor, etc.
 8. _A Day in the Life of a Dinosaur_. Take children on a trip to Dinosaurland! They pantomime actions while teacher tells a story about a dinosaur's day* (See App. 3).

Lesson #12: Directionality Day

Objectives: To internalize directionality, movement patterns and body dynamics.

Materials Needed: Four pieces of paper
Hokey Pokey Music
20 Direction Cards* (See App. 3)
Footprints (cut from paper; right feet are one color, left are another)

Class Outline:

A. Warm-ups* (See App. 1)
B. Activities
1. _Movement._ Walk in circle, change directions and walk the other direction. Now run in a circle, change directions and run the other direction. Stand in a spot and begin exploring directions. Go forward, backward, diagonally, sideways, and turn in place.
2. _Hinges._ Swing arms in big circles. What other body parts can make circles? Hands, feet, fingers. Make circles by laying down on floor and curving body into a circle. Swing head. Add right arm swinging, then left arm swinging, then entire torso. Swing as big as possible and as little as possible side to side. Continue exploring the difference between hinge joints (knees and elbows) which can move forward and backward, and ball and socket joints (hips and shoulders) which can move in almost all directions.
3. _Sequences._ Count in FOUR (1, 2, 3, 4) and have them walk forward for four counts, slide sideways for four counts, hop backward for four counts, then step-turn for four counts. This makes a square. Next, add diagonal movements. It might be helpful to put tape on the floor for diagonal movements.
4. _Partnering._ Pair children. Tell them to chew an imaginary piece of gum. Take it out and put it on hands. Stick hands together so they won't come apart. Face each other and hold hands; move sideways together across floor. This is a great way to learn how to move sideways because they are attached to partner. Hop, boogie, or slide sideways, but they must stick together.
5. _Imagination._ Play an imaginary baseball game. Swing at the pitch and hit a home run, all in slow motion. While traveling from base to base, children will perform a different movement: from home plate to 1st base, walk and turn in circles. From 1st to 2nd base, walk backward. From 3rd base to home plate, walk sideways. After each child has played, change directions. From home plate to 1st base, use swinging motions with body, and then stand on the base making an interesting shape with body. From 1st to 2nd base, make circles with body parts. From 2nd to 3rd base, vibrate body. From 3rd base, hop backward; in slow motion, slide into home plate.
6. _Up and Down._ Show shuffled direction cards like flash cards to children. They stand up or sit down as directed by cards.
7. _Left and Right._ Tape feet patterns on floor in a left, right, left pattern. Children follow patterns saying, "left, right, left, right" etc.

Lesson #13: Dynamics Day

Objectives: To learn the specific dynamics of dance. To develop self-expression while exploring simple body movements that do not have a particular name. To learn that the art of dance goes beyond "jazz, tap and ballet," as children lose intimidations and self-consciousness when interacting with others.

Materials Needed: 4 differently-colored pieces of construction paper

Class Outline:

A.   Warm-ups* (See App. 1)

B.   Activities

    1. _Floating Dynamics._ Follow an imaginary snowflake. Use entire body to 'float it' around room: start from a high level (standing on tip toes) and move through to a low-level (sitting or squatting down). Next, place imaginary snowflake on a different part of the body and repeat. Then, float snowflake to person next to them using different body parts. Finally, smash the snowflake with a percussive movement with any part of the body, i.e., elbow, hand, or foot.

    2. _Punching and Suspension Dynamics._ Children punch quickly and forcefully in air. Punch slowly in air. After mastering punching by themselves, choose a partner for a slow motion punching fight. Aggressors punch in slow motion and victims react by falling to floor and rolling in slow motion.

    3. _Slashing Dynamics._ Arms are straight and "slash" through air. The arms can never bend when slashing. Ask children how they can slash with arms strong enough to get them off ground and into air. Can they slash strong enough to turn in a circle?

    4. _Vibration Dynamics._ Children pretend they are in a big container that a giant picks up and shakes. What would their bodies look like? After they vibrate their bodies, they freeze. Next, vibrate body parts individually: first an arm, a leg, head, etc. Finally, gather them in the corner. Run to the middle of room, make a shape, melt to floor, then run off. Repeat by running to the middle and adding an explosive jump with vocalization, yelling "Pow" or "Bam" before running off.

    5. _Combination Dynamics._ Tape four pieces of colored paper up around room. Children combine two punches, a slash that turns body, and a suspension which melts body to floor (hold leg out and slowly pull it in and melt to the floor). Next, explain that each color represents a dynamic movement. They run to the first color and slash, run to the second color and beat the floor, run to the third color and melt to the floor, run to the fourth color and punch.

    6. _Happy Sunshine._ Several children lay on floor forming a large circle with bodies. Remaining children lay out, flat and straight from circle, as the 'sunshine beams.' Say the following while children do actions: "the sunshine is getting hotter and hotter" (children shake bodies); the sunshine is feeling silly (wiggle bodies while laughing); the sunshine is overpowered by the lightning (percussive movements); thunder is coming! (loud BOOMS with stomping and moving arms outward and inward); rain falls (tip-toe and pitter-patter to original position).

Lesson #14: Feelings Day

Objectives: To develop physical and facial expressions demonstrating various emotions. To increase imagination, improvisation, and confidence. To strengthen sensitivity towards others.

Materials Needed: Music that evokes a variety of emotions
Dolls (or stuffed animals; 1 per child)
Scarves (1 per child)
Instruments (i.e.: drums, tambourines, or maracas; 1 per child)

Class Outline:

A.   Warm-ups* (See App. 1)
B.   Activities

1. _Emotion Locomotion._ Children line up on one side of room. Explain to them that they will be showing different emotions while they move from one side of the room to the other. Call out an emotion. Ask them to move slowly and show emotion with their face and bodies while crossing room. Give a short preparatory statement before each feeling, such as: "It is blistering hot, your clothes are sticking to you and you need a drink of water;" "It's your birthday, and you opened your favorite present; you're bubbling with joy;" "You stubbed your toe and it really hurts."

2. _Musical Moods._ Play a variety of music and talk about how the music makes them feel. Encourage children to move to music.

3. _Hush-A-Bye Baby._ Encourage the nurturing and gentle connection that children can make with a baby. Explain that they will help their baby (doll or stuffed animal) to fall asleep. Put baby on the floor in front of them. Perform the following:
   - Hold 'baby,' singing and swaying from side to side with music
   - Wrap 'baby' in a blanket and twirl around on toes and flat feet
   - Place 'baby' on the floor and tip toe around it
   - Quietly kneel by "baby" and stroke its back and head
   - Whisper "Shhhhhhh" and sing a lullaby

4. _Grumpy Dance._ Declare to the group that you feel very, very grumpy. Discuss the meaning of the word grumpy, and talk about causes of grumpy feelings, and things they can do to make those feelings go away. Have them participate in a 'grumpy dance.' Children use instruments; stomp and grunt loudly. Children gather the grumpy feelings together and blow them away.

5. _Guess What I'm Feeling._ One at a time, a child enters the center of the circle and acts out a feeling. Children guess the feeling, change places and repeat.

6. _Emotion Mirrors._ Pair children. In unison, 'leader' and 'mirror' recite something familiar (i.e., Pledge of Allegiance, the alphabet). Leader changes emotions while mirror imitates. For example, leader speaks in a high-pitched, excited voice to portray anxiety, or with eyes darting back over shoulder to portray fear.

Lesson #15: Finger Play Day

Objectives: To encourage fun while maintaining focus and structure. To develop fine motor skills, listening skills and sequencing. To teach mathematical concepts through movement.

Materials Needed: Popsicle sticks (5 per child)

Class Outline:

A. Warm-ups* (See App. 1)
B. Activities
   1. *Sticky Lollipops.* Give five sticks to each child. Teacher reads rhyme while children act out the finger play* (See App. 3).
   2. *Finger Play Fun.* Teacher reads the rhymes while children act out finger plays: Hands, Worms, Brown Bunny, Five Little Firefighters* (See App. 3).
   3. *Cocoon.* Children play cocoon. Curl up in ball on floor, as if in a cocoon. In order to change into a butterfly, children must wiggle around, stretch, squirm, and roll. Teacher says "butterfly" and they POP out of cocoon and fly around room. Ask "What color butterfly are you?" "Where are you flying?" "Look how high you are!"
   4. *Eency-Weency Spider.* Sing the song normally. Then sing it as the "Itsy-Bitsy Spider" with a small, quiet voice and small finger movements. Then sing it as the "Really Big Spider." Stand and sing it with huge body movements, and loud, deep voices.
   5. *Popcorn.* Children lie on floor. Teacher says, "you are a popcorn kernel in a hot pan. Now sizzle! Now start popping!" Children pantomime actions. All pop up, then girls alone while boys freeze, then reverse.
   6. *Clocks.* Children sit in pike position* (See App. 2) with hands patting legs, slow tempo for big clocks, medium tempo for little clocks and very quickly for watches. Say the chant* (see App. 3).
   7. *Five Little Children.* Teacher reads rhyme in the style of 'Five Little Monkeys' while children act out the finger play* (see App. 3).
   8. *Teddy Bear.* Teacher says the rhyme while children act it out: "Teddy bear, teddy bear, turn around; teddy bear, teddy bear, touch the ground; teddy bear, teddy bear, reach up high; teddy bear, teddy bear, wink one eye; teddy bear, teddy bear, slap your knees; teddy bear, teddy bear, sit down please.
   9. *Ten in a Bed.* Line mats closely together in a row; children lay on them. Sing the rhyme 'Ten in the Bed'* (See App. 3). While singing 'roll over, roll over,' children all roll over and teacher removes the first mat. Child at end who 'fell off' hops up and runs to end of line and lays down. If class size exceeds ten, begin song with the number of children (i.e., "15 in the bed.")
   10. *Ten Little Indians.* Teacher reads the rhyme while children act out the finger play* (see App. 3).

Lesson #16: Food Day

Objectives: To increase listening skills while having fun with food.

Materials Needed: 2 baskets: 1 empty, 1 full of plastic food items (from a play kitchen)
        Lightweight balls
        A sheet
        Many plastic food items
        Obstacle course items: masking tape, hula hoops, 3 cones
        A lemon
        A chocolate bar

Class Outline:

A.   Warm-ups* (See App. 1)

B.   Activities

1. *Food Moves.* Teacher calls out the following foods for children to act out: move like wiggly spaghetti, popping popcorn, a melting popsicle, jiggly jello, sticky peanut butter, rising bread, dripping water, pouring milk, a floppy hotdog, a melting ice cream cone.

2. *Pass the Fruit.* Place baskets at each end of room. Children form line between baskets. Child closest to food chooses one item and passes it to their neighbor. Continue passing. The child at end of row puts item into empty basket. Continue until all food items have been moved from one basket to the other.

3. *Popcorn.* Children hold edges of a sheet and toss lightweight balls onto sheet while making popping sounds with lips.

4. *Food Pass.* Children sit in circle around bucket of plastic food. Each child chooses one food item. As Teacher says, "pass," each child passes item to right and receives item from left. Continue.

5. *Jello in the Bowl.* Children sit in circle to form a 'bowl.' One at a time, they go into the center of circle and wiggle and dance any way they like. Sing the jello song (sung to the tune of 'The Farmer in the Dell'): *Jello in the bowl, jello in the bowl, Weeble, wobble, weeble, wobble, jello in the bowl!* Continue until everyone has had a turn to be the jell-o!

6. *Apple, Apple, Burger!* Play "Duck, Duck, Goose" but use food instead.

7. *Obstacle Course.* Children follow course, set up as the following:
    - On hands and knees, children roll an orange down a designated (taped) pathway;
    - Jump through hula hoop;
    - Toss food from full bucket to empty bucket;
    - Carry food item between legs while hopping;
    - Balance banana on head while walking around cones.

8. *Silly Senses.* Children close eyes. Have them smell the chocolate. Children move bodies how they think the chocolate smells or tastes, such as sweet or thick. Then smell and taste the lemon. Teacher says, "how does it make your body move? Show those qualities in your face, right down to your toes!

Lesson #17: Frog Day

Objectives: To develop creativity and imagination, strengthen mind/body coordination, develop endurance, and increase flexibility and agility.

Materials Needed: Masking tape
Several lily pads (hula hoops)
A sheet
A stuffed frog

Class Outline:

A. Warm-ups* (See App. 1)
B. Activities
1. _Leap Frog._ Children form a line, squatting on hands and knees. The child at end of line straddle-jumps over each child then gets in place at front of line. The next child at the back of line straddle-jumps to front and gets in place at front. Continue.
2. _Tadpole._ Children begin as an egg in pond and pantomime as teacher tells story* (See App. 3). Modify by stopping music during narration and having children freeze, or do movements in slow motion.
3. _Green Speckled Frogs._ Teacher reads rhyme 'Green Speckled Frogs' below. Change rhyme to reflect number of children in class. Have 'frogs' (children) squat on 'log' (masking tape line). Read rhyme and have first frog jump off log. Repeat until there are no more frogs. Children call out number of frogs left on log each time.
    "_(10)_ green and speckled frogs, sat on a speckled log,
    Eating some most delicious bugs, Yum, yum!
    One jumped into the pool, where it was nice and cool,
    Then there were _(9)_ green speckled frogs. Glub, glub!"
4. _Frog Pond._ Set out enough lily pads (hula hoops) that there will be a few children who will not have one. Children hop around outside the hula hoops. Say, "RIBBIT RIBBIT;" children hop to a lily pad. There will be more than one child on a pad. Teacher removes one pad then says: "Little frog, little frog please hop off my lily pad." Children hop off pad and around room again. Continues until there is only one lily pad left with all the frogs on it.
5. _Frog Hop._ As music plays, children squat down, hold ankles and jump like a frog.
6. _Toss the Frog._ Use a parachute or sheet and have the children hold the edges. Help them toss a stuffed frog on sheet. When music begins, sheet should be flat on ground and frog lying in the middle. Children listen to the music and move the frog by lifting the sheet up and down, and rotating while holding sheet in a circle.
7. _Over the Froggie._ Place stuffed frog in middle of room. Children line up at one side of room. When music starts, run across room and leap over frog without stepping on it.

Lesson #18: Fun Day

Objectives: To enjoy fun activities that encourage movement, creativity, and following instructions.

Materials Needed: A marionette doll
Differently-colored felt squares (several of each color)
A teddy bear
Blocks (several per child)
Scarves (1 per child)
Several Hula Hoops
Balls (1 per child)

Class Outline:

A.   Warm-ups* (See App. 1)
B.   Activities
  1. _Marionette._ Children pretend they are marionettes. Show a real marionette to help them understand the activity. Pretend a puppeteer is on the ceiling holding them up. Children pantomime while teacher reads narrative* (See App. 3).
  2. _Felt Square Twister._ Place felt squares around room. Music plays while children dance. Teacher gives various directions for children to follow. For example, "put your right hand on red. Stick your nose on blue. Attach your ear to yellow. Sit on green. Put your big toe on orange."
  3. _Please Pass the Teddy!_ Children line up. One child holds a stuffed animal under chin. Without using hands, pass animal to the next child in line. Continue until it reaches last child. Time them. Have boys do it, then girls.
  4. _Build a Tower._ Children build tower by picking up blocks with elbows, chin, feet.
  5. _Scarf Walk._ Children put a scarf over head. Walk slowly and carefully, keeping scarf in place; walk backward and turn slowly; move scarf to different body parts: elbow, shoulder, hand, etc. How else can they balance it? Continue walking.
  6. _Hula Hoop Hustle._ Scatter hula hoops around room. As music plays, children travel around room using a locomotor movement* (See App. 4). When music stops, teacher calls out specific directions, such as: "put right hand in a hula hoop. Stand with left foot in a hula hoop. Put your head in a hula hoop!" Continue.
  7. _Opposites!_ Standing in circle, children do opposite of the word said. For example, teacher says, "sit," and children stand. Say, "be very quiet," children scream loudly.
  8. _Telephone._ Children sit in circle and whisper a message from person to person. When message gets back to its original source, it has invariably changed, usually with humorous results. Repeat. Modification: children pass along a movement.
  9. _Hopscotch._ Place squares in a hopscotch pattern. Children line up at beginning of pattern and teacher sits at other end. One at a time, children follow pattern. When they reach end, teacher tosses them a ball to catch. They carry ball with them to end of line. The next time they go through hopscotch, they toss ball back to teacher.

Lesson #19: Game Day

Objectives: To enhance listening skills and memory through sharing spaces and following directions.

Materials Needed: Carpet squares (1 per child)
Masking tape
Beanbags (1 per child)

Class Outline:

A.   Warm-ups* (See App. 1)
B.   Activities
1. *Information Station.* To be beneficial, games must be geared to suit the abilities of the age group. Modify competitive games to create a spirit of cooperation and non-elimination. Keep groups small to minimize waiting for turns; make as few rules as possible, and keep them simple. Games are easily learned when children begin with simple activities and progress to more difficult ones. Each of the following is described in steps, from simple to more complicated variations.
2. *Here Today.* This game helps children learn each other's names. For younger children, use first names only. For older children, use first and last names. Everyone begins by standing in a circle. Say the following, inserting each child's name on by one, continuing around circle: *(Child's Name) is here today, (Child's Name) is here today. Turn around, then sit down, (Child's Name) is here today!*
3. *Crack the Egg.* Pair children; one is the "Egg," curling entire body into tight egg shape holding arms around knees, and the other is the "Mother Hen," gently rolling egg around room with hands. Teacher says "Crack!" and Egg cracks open with arms and legs extended. Then Egg and Mother Hen switch places. Repeat.
4. *Here We Come!* Designate a line in middle of room with tape. Divide children into two groups and line up facing each other on opposite sides of room. Groups chant* (See App. 3) while Group 1 walks to line. Group 1 pantomimes an animal, object or occupation while Group 2 guesses. When Group 2 has guessed correctly, Group 1 hops on one foot back to original spot. If Group 1 children are tagged by Group 2 children, they switch teams.
5. *Musical Squares.* Each child sits on carpet square in a circle. Stand and walk around circle when music starts. When music stops, stand on square quickly! Teacher removes one square, starts music, and children resume walking. Next time music stops, someone needs to share a square! Continue until all but one square is removed. How many fit on one square?
6. *Ring Around the Rosy.* Using masking tape, make a large circle on floor. While chanting the rhyme, children walk around circle, staying on tape. Balance beanbags on heads. Move beanbags to other body parts and repeat.
7. *Simon Says.* Children stand facing teacher. Teacher says, "Simon says _____," and performs an action; children imitate. If teacher gives direction without saying "Simon says," children should not imitate action. If they do, they sit.
8. *Other Suggestions.* Follow the Leader, Mother May I, Red Light Green Light.

Lesson #20: Gymnastics Day

Objectives: To help children develop body awareness, and learn specific gymnastics positions. To improve strength, flexibility and endurance. To learn balance and hand-eye coordination.

Materials Needed: Masking tape
Bean bags
Balloons
Three Hula Hoops
Several empty plastic soda bottles
Ladder

Class Outline:

A. Warm-ups* (See App. 1)
B. Activities
1. _Practice gymnastic positions*_. (See App. 2) Lunge, squat, pike, straddle, v-sit, straight-body, sit-ups, hop, jump, skip, gallop, butterfly, birdie-perch, soldier jump, tuck jump. After mastering these on floor, move to balance beam.
2. _Balance Beam_. Put masking tape on floor in a long line. Children walk forward, backward, side-to-side, turning. Put bean bags on balance beam and walk or step-kick over bean bags. Try bunny hops. Jump or leap off end of beam tucked up with legs spread wide in straddle or making ¼, ½, ¾ or full turns.
3. _Animal walks*_. (See App. 2) Learn crab walk, horsie kick, stink bug walk (hands and feet straight and extended to floor; then walk.) Then, play leap frog. Children form a line, squatting on hands and knees. The child at the end of line straddle-jumps over each child until reaching front. Repeat.
4. _Balloon time_. Free time; keep the balloons in air using hands, feet and head.
5. _Hula Hoops_. Teacher holds hula hoop; children push balloons through. Toss bean bags through hoop. Put three hoops on floor in a line; hop in and out with both feet together. Keep hoops on floor, and put both hands inside hoops, while feet stay on outside; children hop around hoop (introduction to cartwheels).
6. _Let's Go!_ Put masking tape on floor in waves, zig zags, or circles. Children move along lines with or without a blindfold. Lie down inside or around shapes.
7. _Charades_. One child acts out an animal or object. Others guess what it is. For example, flamingo: stand on one leg on beam while bending other leg so sole of foot touches inside of knee of standing leg. Use arms for balance. Airplane: stand on one leg, arms to sides, raise back leg up as high as possible, keeping head up.
8. _Go Between_. Place empty bottles upright in a line, leaving space between them. Children weave between bottles without knocking them down.
9. _Cross Crawling_. Lay ladder flat on floor. Children crawl across ladder putting feet and hands on alternating rungs.
10. _Color it!_ Give each child a piece of colored material. Call out directions for different colors: 'If your material is red, go stand by the door.' 'If green, lay on your stomach.' 'If yellow, fly around the room.' Continue.

Lesson #21: Happy Day

Objectives: To learn to take turns through activities which encourage and improve peer interaction.

Materials Needed: 6 colored scarves
12 differently-colored felt squares
Box Cube* (See App. 3)
Colored Index Cards* (See App. 4)

Class Outline:

A. Warm-ups* (See App. 1)
B. Activities
   1. _Information Station_. Formations can be helpful in managing a class. Although difficult, they provide great variety. For example, a circle is a challenging formation for children to master. Have children stand with hands on hips, elbows extended. Children come together so that their elbows touch their friend's elbows, forming a circle. Then rotate circle to right, then to left.
   2. _Rainbow Dance_. Children stand in circle. Everyone will have a turn to dance a rainbow. Lay six scarves in middle of circle and choose six children to begin. Turn on music and let six children dance with scarves while others hold hands in circle around them. When finished, choose six others and repeat. Using too many scarves becomes confusing. Watch movements of each child; point out specifics.
   3. _What Makes You Happy?_ Ask children one at a time what makes them happy; i.e., riding a bike, eating ice cream, swimming. Class acts out each suggestion.
   4. _Roll Over_. Lay out twelve felt squares in a row. Children lay down in a row and sing, "10 in a bed, and the little one said, roll over, roll over. So they all rolled over and one fell out, 9 kids in the bed and the little one said, roll over, roll over... etc." All children roll over, then child at end pops up and runs to end of row. Repeat.
   5. _The Happy Cube_. Sit in a circle and have each child throw the cube into center one at a time. Perform song or dance indicated on cube.
   6. _If You're Happy_. Children stand in circle. Discuss how we show feelings through gestures and expressions: cold, itchy, scared, happy, surprised, etc. Sing song, "If You're Happy and You Know It." Begin with 'clap your hands,' then with subsequent verses, substitute the following directions: stamp your feet, jump and yell, shiver and shake, melt to the floor, burst in the air.
   7. _Colored Index Cards_. Use Index Cards. If children can read, let them read card. If not, teacher reads card for them. Perform movement indicated on card.
   8. _Happy Sunshine_. Several children lay on floor forming a large circle with bodies. Remaining children lay out, flat and straight from circle, as the 'sunshine beams.' Say the following while children do actions: "the sunshine is getting hotter and hotter" (children shake bodies); "the sunshine is feeling silly" (wiggle bodies while laughing); "the sunshine is sad" (curl or turn on tummies with sad faces); "the sunshine is going to bed" (group rolls into large moon shape on floor); "sunshine is awake again" (scurry into sunshine position again).

Lesson #22: Imitation Day

Objectives: To identify objects and mimic them with body movements. To connect thoughts to actions while developing coordination and improving listening skills.

Materials Needed: Tactile items: bowl of Jell-O, rag doll, packet of seeds, rubber band

Class Outline:

A. Warm-ups* (See App. 1)
B. Activities
1. *Wheelbarrow Races*. One child walks on his hands while another child is holding his feet. The child who is walking on hands must keep body straight.
2. *Imitate*. Children make bodies look like a:
    - *Puppy*. Excited, wagging 'tail' in air; tired, slumping shoulders.
    - *Camel*. Hunch back with head hanging low. How high can you make the hump?
    - *Spider*. 'Spray' crawlers with pretend bug spray; they fall on back and kick legs.
    - *Snake*. Slither around floor; coil up body; strike.
    - *Elephant*. Lumber around slowly, swaying a 'trunk;' run excitedly in a big herd.
    - *Peacock*. Proudly walk with legs extended, toe-heel. Keep head in the air. Extended hands straight out in back for feathers.
    - *Kangaroo*. Pretend feet are glued together. Bounce around room.
3. *Visual Connections*. Show children items and have them pantomime the following:
    - *Bowl of Jell-O*. Make bodies look like wobbly texture.
    - *Rag Doll*. Floppy heads and floppy arm movements while sitting on floor.
    - *Seeds*. Discuss what happens when you plant a seed. Children squat in 'dirt' then slowly grow into a beautiful flower. Move arms around to look like petals.
    - *Rubber band*. Stretch bodies; slowly open arms; clap them shut quickly. Attach pretend rubber band to foot and hand and stretch it. Then hand to head, and bottom to wrist.
4. *Guessing Game*. Teacher pantomimes following actions while children guess: cut grass, climb ladder, fish, dust, sew, climb stairs, butterfly, make a bed, paint a wall, rake leaves, wash car, sweep, roller skate, and dig.
5. *Make a Flower*. Children sit in circle with feet touching in middle. Curl up with arms around knees in a crack-the-egg position. Ask children what color flower they would like to make. Say, "open the red flower." Everyone rolls onto back and kicks legs in air. Say, "close the flower," and return to crack-the-egg position. Repeat until every child chooses a color for the flower.
6. *Look at Me!* Children creatively perform actions while teacher says the following: "How would your body look if you were walking on the clouds? If you're house is on fire? If your leg is broken? If you are up to your waist in water? If you're in the middle of a scary tornado? If you're hiking up the mountain with a heavy backpack? If you're riding on a crowded, bumpy bus?"
7. *Cross-Country Race*. Children imitate a cross-country runner as teacher reads story* (See App. 3).

Lesson #23: Indian Day

Objectives: To increase understanding of geometric concepts and level changes through child's play. To develop coordination, body control and imagination.

Materials Needed: Teepee* (see App. 3)
Lumme sticks
Tambourines (1 per child)
Stick horses (1 per child)
5-ft pliable cotton rope (1 per pair)
Large feathers (1 per child)
A sheet
A rubber snake
Traditional Indian music (optional)

Class Outline:

A. Warm-ups* (See App. 1)
B. Activities
1. *Teepee.* Have children help set up a teepee in middle of room. Discuss Indians and show pictures.
2. *War Paint.* Pair children. Each child pantomimes putting war paint on their partner's face. Encourage the use of different shapes: with fingers, draw triangles, circles, squares, lines and dots on cheeks.
3. *Move Around the Teepee.* Children tap lumme sticks together while traveling around teepee.
4. *Soar and Swoop.* Children pantomime while teacher says the following: "Spread your wings like eagles and soar high above the water! Get ready, we're going to swoop... ready... go! Down, down, down. Soar close to the water. Skim over the waves until you see a fish. Dip down and catch it! Now fly back into the sky!"
5. *Indian Dance.* Encourage children to do an Indian dance, jumping and hopping while playing their tambourines.
6. *Indian Pony.* Give each child a stick horse. They 'ride' around room.
7. *Indian Rope.* Pair children; give each pair one end of a rope. Play tug of war.
8. *Feather Dancing.* Give each child a feather to 'feather dance' with. While music plays, keep the feather in air by blowing it. Next, throw entire bag of feathers in air. Children gather up their own little bunches.
9. *Toss the Snake!* Using a sheet as a parachute, children toss and catch snake.
10. *Pass the Snake!* Children sit in circle and pass snake while music plays. Whoever is holding it when music stops gets bitten and lays down. Repeat until everyone is laying down.
11. *Canoe Adventure.* Children pantomime the following: Get into canoe (sit in a row); row ores at same time; see an animal (put hand to forehead as if seeing something); take out bow and arrows and shoot animal (uh-oh, missed!); row through raging, bumpy rapids; row through a rain storm; row to shore, get off boat; fish from shore; carry fish back to tents and sit around fire.

Lesson #24: Lumme Sticks Day

Objectives: To develop sequencing skills and auditory factors, such as awareness, perception, and memory.

Materials Needed: Lumme sticks (12-in. long dowel rods; 2 per child)
                      Balloons

Class Outline:

A.   Warm-ups* (See App. 1)
B.   Activities
     1. *Pointing Game.* Give each child a lumme stick and point to each of the following body parts: fingers, feet, knees, elbows, chin, tongue, eyebrows, stomach, legs, arms, mouth, eyes, nose, shoulders, hips, hands, head.
     2. *Tapping.* Give each child two lumme sticks and stand in large circle. Tap sticks in the following ways: high in air; low, while marching in place; tapping and turning; pull them into chest; tapping ends together while holding horizontally. Hold sticks vertically in each hand and push them straight out in front of body.
     3. *Partners.* Children face each other in pairs. Tap sticks by themselves first: slowly, quickly, up high, down low. Hold onto sticks while bending body to one side, then other side. Tap behind back. Children *slowly and gently* tap each other's lumme stick. One at a time at first, then both sticks together.
     4. *Balloons.* Children keep balloons in air using sticks.
     5. *Sequencing.* Teacher does the following sequence several times: tap sticks high in the sky / tap sticks like a drum on floor (body is squatting) / hold sticks into chest and turn around in a quick circle / make a Martian (put both sticks on top of head, sticking out like antennae). Do sequence with children. Then children do sequence with only verbal cues from teacher. Modification: reverse sequence.
     6. *Silly Sticks.* While music plays, do the following with sticks: tap together to each side of body, kick legs while tapping sticks, shake sticks in air (no contact, no noise), slow stretching with sticks, criss-cross sticks (arms open, then cross over, then open back up again), sit down tapping on floor, criss-cross on floor, tap knees, tap feet & toes, wind the sticks (hold them horizontally and roll them around each other over and over), make a fire (scrape sticks together), jumping jacks with sticks.
     7. *Musical Sticks.* Pretend to play musical instruments: flute, violin, guitar, trombone, trumpet while marching.
     8. *Hopscotch.* Group children into threes. Two children each hold two ends of sticks, forming a square while squatting. They open sticks wide enough so third person can jump in the middle. Then, stick holders pull sticks into center so third person must straddle jump sticks. Continue.
     9. *What Do You Hear?* Children lie on floor with eyes closed. Each child takes turns tapping a rhythm and class repeats. Continue.
     10. *Water-Skiing.* Lay sticks on floor and stand on them. Pretend to water-ski by bending, twisting, hunching down low, squatting, jumping, springing and bolting.

Lesson #25: Motion Day

Objectives: To increase self-esteem, confidence, and imagination through movement.

Materials Needed: Four cones
Items to hang from ceiling (curtains, streamers, balloons)
Items to go over and under (ropes, poles, hula hoops, blankets, climbing equipment)

Class Outline:

A.   Warm-ups* (See App. 1)
B.   Activities

1. _Motion Mania_. Brainstorm ways to move across a space: slither, tiptoe, roll, prance, gallop, spin, cartwheel, skate, fly, swim, walk, crawl, run, skip, jump, stomp, hop, leap, slide, scoot, and crouch. Children line up and teacher calls out a movement. Children use that movement to cross room. Demonstrate locomotor movements as needed. Try pathways, such as zigzag, curves, spirals, wandering or diagonal. Try directions, such as forward, backward, and sideways. Try levels, such as low, middle, and high.

2. _Long, Long Jump_. Pair children. Pairs take turns jumping to end of room. One child broad jumps as far as possible while the second child waits. Then, second child begins their broad jump where the first child lands. Continue.

3. _Musical Storybook_. Teacher is the 'book' and encircles two children with arms. Teacher tells a very brief story (ten seconds), then opens the 'book' (arms) and says "Once Upon a time!" Children _dance_ (not pantomime) to story the teacher told. After a few minutes, teacher says, "The End!" and closes arms around same two children. They sit down. Repeat with two new children. Story ideas:
   - _Princess goes to pond, finds a frog, kisses him, and turns him into a prince._
   - _Knight on horse goes into the forest and finds a dragon._
   - _Pirate digs for buried treasure and sails away on ship._
   - _Scientist working in a lab creates a dancing robot._

4. _Move it!_ Everyone stands in center of room. Four cones are set up in corners of room. Travel from cone to cone using a locomotion skill* (See App. 4). Repeat.

5. _What if?_ Ask children, "how would you move if the floor was..." (then say the following one by one as they act it out): sticky because glue was spilled on it; sandy because a truck poured sand all over it; bouncy because someone dropped 100 rubber balls on it; slippery because it is all ice; prickly because someone put thorny roses all over it.

6. _Move on Through_. Hang light objects at different heights from ceiling like a maze. Children freely bump balloons, move through streamers, follow curtains, etc. Try a game of Follow the Leader or Simon Says.

7. _Over and Under Pairs_. Explore 'over' and 'under' using items that enable children to walk, run, climb and jump over and under. Use Action Cards* (See App. 4).

Lesson #26: Movement Day

Objectives: To develop observation and concentration skills through unified movement.

Materials Needed: A wide variety of music
                      Dress up props
                      Masking tape
                      Large ball for each child
                      Large sheet
                      Scarves (1 per child)
                      Large, thick quilt

Class Outline:

A.   Warm-ups* (See App. 1)

B.   Activities

1. *Moving to Music*. Children dance to a variety of music: marching, waltzes, Latin, current hits, and classical. The greater the variety, the better the activity will be. Use scarves or dress-up props that encourage movement. Be careful about demonstrating too much; the goal is for children to create their own movements.

2. *Log Roll*. Children roll like logs with bodies stretched out tall, legs together, and hands together high above head.

3. *Jump the Brook*. Mark a 'brook' on the floor with two strips of masking tape, placed close together at one end and further apart at the other. Discuss correct ways to jump and land: to jump - bend knees and hips, swing arms, hard, push off ground with balls of feet. To land - bend knees and hips for 'quiet landings,' and land on balls of feet. Jump over brook, starting at narrow end, working way to the end.

4. *Skipping*. Learn the basic process of skipping. Give each child a ball to hold tightly with both arms. Standing in place, children raise one knee to bump the ball. Then, raise other knee to bump ball again. Practice this movement repeatedly. Then pretend there is a strong wind blowing them from behind. Continue raising knees to ball and add forward movement.

5. *Under the Sheet*. Two teachers hold corners of sheet. Children lay on floor under sheet. Teachers lift arms and flick sheet upward to create a canopy that balloons over children. The canopy will keep its shape for a few seconds as arms lower. Repeat.

6. *Scarf Sharing*. Pair children; give each pair a scarf. Children face each other and each hold two corners of scarf. Take turns mirroring each other. Move slowly and smoothly together. Move from side to side, high and low, toward each other and apart, all around. Be careful; do not pull or stretch the scarves.

7. *Jumping on the Bed*. Children love to jump! Lay quilt on floor for children to jump on. There are many different ways they can jump: high, low, pointy, graceful, spinning, touching knees, straddling legs with a friend, clapping hands.

8. *Show Me Your Moves!* Teacher says, "Everyone show me a movement that is: (call out the following one by one) sharp, curvy, loopy, bumpy, straight, zigzag, long, short, flat tall, round, lumpy." Children move the way they feel portrays that word.

Lesson #27: Museum Day

Objectives: To discover the concept of positive and negative space and use it to create interesting body shapes and inter-relationships. To work as a group to create an image through body sculpting techniques. To explore body shapes, physical contact and trust.

Materials Needed: Scarves (1 per child)
Paintbrushes (1 per child)
Sponges (1 per child)
Stuffed animals (1 per child)

Class Outline:

A. Warm-ups* (See App. 1)
B. Activities
1. *Information Station.* Teacher says, "Today we will visit a museum. What do you find?" Discuss aspects of statues. Teacher demonstrates different statue poses while children slowly walk around and examine the 'statue.' Repeat, giving children different positional ideas.
2. *Dancing Statues.* Play music while children dance. When music stops, children freeze in whatever pose they are in. Repeat. After children master individual statues, form a statue with partner and freeze when music stops.
3. *Positive and Negative Space** (See App. 2). Explain that body mass is 'positive' space, and empty space that the body encloses is 'negative' space or 'holes' (i.e.: positive space in a donut is the actual donut; negative space is the hole). Children strike a pose that will produce as many negative spaces, or holes, as possible. Freeze. While holding positions, point out negative space (holes) that can be found in each child's statue. Explore this activity on high, middle and low levels.
4. *Scarf Sculptures.* Each child makes statues using a scarf.
5. *Group Sponge Sculpture.* One at a time, children place sponges on floor to make a sculpture. Sponge can be tall, flat, or on its side. When sculpture is complete, children tell what they think it looks like.
6. *Symmetrical and Asymmetrical.* Introduce concepts of symmetry: draw an imaginary line down center of body, both sides are exactly the same, and asymmetry: the same imaginary line produces two different sides. Children form several different symmetrical shapes with body. Then form asymmetrical shapes.
7. *Partner Sculpting.* Pair children. One is 'Sculptor,' and the other is 'Clay.' Clay is relaxed and moves in any way Sculptor places them. Clay freezes and holds that position until moved again by Sculptor. Trade places and repeat.
8. *Group Sculpture.* As music plays, children dance. When music stops, children attach themselves to each other, forming one large group sculpture. Repeat.
9. *Paint Your Own Masterpiece!* Give each child a paintbrush. Stand by wall and pretend to paint a picture. One by one, they tell the class what they painted.
10. *Animal Sculptures.* Children place animals in center of room forming an animal sculpture. Then children copy the animal statue by making an identical human statue with their own bodies.

Lesson #28: Music Day

Objectives: To increase recognition of different musical styles, rhythms, and tempos.

Materials Needed: Paper (1 sheet per child)
        Crayons (1 per child)
        Various music types
        Scarves (1 per child)
        Items to suspend (wooden blocks, plastic bottles, cardboard rolls, pans)
        Items to strike with (wooden or metal spoons)
        Recording of everyday sounds

Class Outline:

A.   Warm-ups* (See App. 1)
B.   Activities
   1. *Drawing Music*. Children sit on floor. Give children a piece of paper and crayons. Play music without talking; have them draw what they hear. When song is over, hold up each child's musical drawing; have them explain their picture.
   2. *Feel the Music*. Play a different variety of music (jazzy, classical, popular, folksy). Encourage children to move bodies while standing, laying down, or sitting. Next, add props such as scarves. Encourage creativity.
   3. *Streamers*. Give each child a scarf for each hand. Make scarves fly in different ways: high, low, fast, slow, and crazy. Walk fast or slow, high and low. Make shapes in air or on floor with streamers. Keep streamers close to body, then far away from body.
   4. *Sound Line*. Suspend objects securely (blocks, bottles, etc.) Children use different objects to strike items with, such as wooden and metal spoons. Discuss the different sounds they make.
   5. *What Do You Hear?* Children lie on floor with eyes closed. Each child takes turns tapping a rhythm and class repeats. Continue. Get up and dance the sounds.
   6. *Balloon Ballad*. Children keep balloons in air while music plays.
   7. *Name That Tune*. Play or hum a few notes of a favorite song. See if the children can name the song. Give them more notes if needed.
   8. *Determine the Dynamics!* Teacher squats in middle as children sing and dance around room. When teacher is low, children's singing and movements are soft and slow. As teacher rises, children's singing and movements increase in volume and tempo.
   9. *Body Alphabet*. Children stand and sing the "ABC" song, while forming each letter with their body. Then, let children call out words one by one, and class spells out the words with their body.
  10. *Sing Along*. Choose a song all children know. First, squinch bodies in tight, tiny balls and sing song very softly. Then, stand on tiptoes with arms big and sing song loudly. Then vary speed, doing it slowly, then fast.

Lesson #29: Nursery Rhyme Day

**Objectives:** To explore locomotion, balance, and rhythm patterns through nursery rhymes.

**Materials Needed:** 7' (2x4) wood piece
Masking tape
Beanbags (1 per child)
Bells (or maracas; 1 per child)
Humpty Dumpty (white lunch bag stuffed with paper, tied at top, with Humpty face drawn on it)
Candlesticks (1 per child; votives or toilet paper tubes)

Class Outline:

A. Warm-ups* (See App. 1)
B. Nursery Rhymes. Before each activity, say the full rhyme together* (see App. 3).
1. _Jack and Jill._ Show children now to roll and do somersaults. Encourage them to 'tumble down the hill.'
2. _London Bridge._ Place a 2x4 in center of room. Children take turns walking across 'London Bridge.' Stay close to them for help and support.
3. _Ring Around the Rosey._ Using masking tape, make a large circle on floor. While chanting the rhyme, children walk around circle, staying on tape. Balance beanbags on heads. Move beanbags to other body parts and repeat.
4. _Ride a Cock Horse._ Children gallop across floor. Repeat, adding a free-style dance. With bells, jiggle the 'bells on her toes.'
5. _Pussycat, Pussycat._ Children locomote in a straight line across room with a sneaky, tip-toe movement. Repeat, following a winding course. While saying, "I frightened a little mouse under her chair," ask children to quickly dash and pounce.
6. _Little Miss Muffet._ Discuss 'tuffet' as a low seat, and "curds and whey" as food similar to cottage cheese or yogurt. Have children locomote across room, first skipping, then creeping, then running. Miss Muffet sits in the middle of the room; children are spiders and scare her.
7. _Humpty Dumpty._ Set Humpty Dumpty on a table. Children take turns throwing a beanbag and knocking him off the 'wall.' Next, 'king's horses' (children) do a side-slide movement with a partner, facing each other holding hands. Then pretend they are eggs, curling body round and tight. Roll around, and then fall, broken and jagged shapes on floor. Then, teacher says, "Then along came his mother and 'clickety-clack' she put him together and set him back" while walking around room picking children up into a standing position.
8. _Jack Be Nimble._ Demonstrate 'jumping over the candlestick' when the word "jump" is said in poem. Repeat several times, observing how feet, arms, and knees move. Give each child a candlestick and spread out to practice jumping.
9. _Sing a Song of Sixpence._ Children pantomime actions while teacher reads rhyme.

Lesson #30: Obstacle Course Day

Objectives: To build endurance and stamina through aerobic activity. To refine locomotor skills and develop memory through sequencing.

Materials Needed: Obstacle course items as appropriate

Class Outline:

A. Warm-ups* (See App. 1)
B. Activities
1. _Obstacle Course._ Put together an obstacle course depending on the age of the children. Use the following suggestions:
    - Slide down a slide, crawl through a tunnel, push a beach ball with nose while crawling between two jump ropes laid out on floor to make a pathway, zigzag with wheelbarrow around cones.
    - Put ladder (or shower rod with balloons tied for steps) on floor, step through, flick balloons with toes, use a bat to scoot a ball around cones in a zigzag pattern, do frog jumps from each carpet square, pick up a bean bag and throw it in bucket.
    - Tie jump ropes to chairs (or cones), children crawl under one, over one, under one, over one. Someone holds a hula hoop and children throw a ball through, hop on one foot, slide down slide.
    - Lay jump rope out in a squiggly line. Children walk on rope while trying not to fall off, set up cones with little balls balancing on top of cones. Children knock balls off with bat, jump over 3 bean bags, crawl through tunnel.
    - Human Wheelbarrow Races: one child walks on his hands while another child is holding his feet. The child who is walking on his hands must keep body straight.
    - Put bean bags between legs and hop to end of room, touch floor and run back to next person in line. Continue until each person has done this in both lines.
    - Put hula hoops on floor and hop through them to the end, camel walk back: walk on hands and feet with both extended and straight.
    - Use playground equipment such as swings, slides, wagons and tricycles.
    - Use masking tape to provide challenging pathways. Tape a pathway in a straight, angular, or curved pattern. Children move or push an object (ball, beanbag, etc.) along the pathway.
    - Stretch two ropes along floor and encourage children to walk or run between, over, along ropes.
    - Children start by walking along a thick piece of masking tape on floor. Then progress to a 2x4 on floor. Next, raise the 2x4 up onto some bricks. Gradually introduce walking along a balance beam, placed one foot above ground, first with support and then without support.
    - Children jump down steps, or jump with both feet over a tire, hopping over a tire on one foot at a time, or jumping over a line taped to floor.
    - Place five bottles upright randomly around room. Children move one at a time, between and around bottles without touching them. Weave in and out.

Lesson #31: Opposite Day

Objectives: To learn about opposites. To explore sizes, shapes, pathways, movements and level changes as they identify contrasting qualities.

Materials Needed: A raw potato (or Mr. Potato Head)
Stuffed animals (1 per child)
Punch balls (1 per child)
Masking Tape
A sheet
A rope
A ball

Class Outline:

A.   Warm-ups* (See Appendix 1)
B.   Activities
1. _Information Station._ Children stand with feet hip distance apart, arms stretched out to sides. Discuss meaning of the word 'opposite. Say, "Stretch as _big_ as you can, then as _small_ as you can... be _soft_ like jello, then be _stiff_ like a tree... be a branch blowing in the _gentle_ wind, then, in the _strong_ wind."
2. _Hot Potato._ Children sit in opposite position in a circle: boy-girl-boy-girl, sit-stand-sit-stand, or face-in-face-out-face-in-face-out. They play hot potato with a real potato by passing it around first slowly, then fast. Modification: each child holds a spoon and passes the potato from spoon to spoon.
3. _Pick it Up._ As music plays, children stand with feet apart, holding a stuffed animal. Drop animal between feet. Then, keeping legs straight, bend at waist to pick up animal. Continue, emphasizing that 'up' and 'down' are opposite directions.
4. _Punch Balls._ Children use a punch ball to follow the dynamics of the music.
5. _Size and Shape._ Children circle arms, hands, feet, head and hips in small circles, then big circles. Walk on tiptoes with tiny steps, then large steps. Walk in a straight line, then a zigzag pattern. Follow a masking tape pathway on the floor.
6. _Parachute._ Make sheet ripple gently, then shake it hard. Hold high, then low.
7. _Over and Under._ Explore 'over' and 'under' with a rope. Lay rope on floor, and children walk over it. Then two children hold it while others walk under it. What other props can you find in the room to demonstrate these opposites? Have them walk, run, climb and jump over and under.
8. _Ball Toss._ Children sit in a circle. Teacher holds ball and says first half of a pair of opposites. The ball is tossed and the person who catches it must call out the other half of the pair of opposites. Teacher says "hot" and child replies "cold."
9. _Pantomime._ Divide children into two groups, facing each other. Each half pantomimes opposites: one group pushes an imaginary object while other group pulls object. Switch. One group stands on tip-toes with arms raised, reaching for the sky, while other group squats down on floor. Switch. Children lay on floor, alternating one on back, one on tummy. Teacher says, "Roll!" and simultaneously, all children flip-flop on ground.

Lesson #32: Pantomime Day

Objectives: To learn creative play and mime. Listen and be open to the children's ideas. Have fun!

Materials Needed: Paper plates (1 per child)

White crepe paper streamers (1 per child; cut in 2' strips or white Kleenex)

Class Outline:

A.   Warm-ups* (See App. 1)
B.   Activities

1. *Winter*. Talk about winter. What do people do in winter? Play music and call out following ideas for children to pantomime: falling snowflakes, walk through snow piled high on ground, sledding, melt into a big puddle on floor, make a snowman, throw snowballs in slow and fast motion, shovel snow, pull sleds, twirl snowflakes.

2. *Animals*. Act out different farm animals with sounds: cow, chicken, dog, cat, pig.

3. *Shoemaker*. Pretend to be a shoemaker. What does a shoemaker do? With music, call out ideas: cut out a shoe from leather, stitch a shoe with a needle, pound a shoe with a hammer, dust hands off on pants when shoe is finished.

4. *Skating*. With barefeet, children use the paper plates as ice-skates.

5. *I'm a Helper*. Children pantomime being different types of helpers: housekeeper - wash dishes, dust, sew, sweep, making beds. Gardener - mow grass, plant flowers, water plants, rake leaves. Fisherman - go in a boat, bait a hook, fish, reel in line.

6. *Farmer*. Talk about a farmer. What does a farmer do? With music, call out ideas: plant seeds, pick fruit from tall trees, milk cows, close barn windows before storm, churn butter, plow field, gather vegetables, feed chickens, ride horse, chop wood.

7. *Dance of the Snowflake*. As music plays, children dance with streamers or Kleenex.

8. *It's Magic*. Teacher uses a pretend magic wand and turns children into a variety of things. Pantomime actions and movements: race car racing, popcorn popping, pancake being flipped, seed growing, tree in a big windstorm, rubber-band snapping, ball bouncing, rag doll flopping around, butter melting, egg being beaten, lawn mower mowing, bowl of jell-O wiggling.

9. *Creative Time*. Children sit along wall. One at a time, children move to center and pantomime the following: playing a video game, getting dressed, feeding your cat, cuddle up in a sleeping bag, riding on a train, driving in a car and missing the exit.

10. *The Visitor*. Read story* (See App. 3) while children perform the actions.

11. *Rhyme Charades*. Everyone sits in circle. Teacher says, "I am thinking of a word that rhymes with dog." One child goes to center of circle. They do NOT say the word, but pantomime their guess. For example, they may pantomime 'frog' by jumping around on floor. Other children guess what center child is pantomiming. Continue until word is guessed. (Examples: 'Oat'– boat, coat, goat, float, note, tote; 'Air'– bear, wear, stair, chair, mare, dare, fair, glare, hair, pear, square.)

12. *Walk the Dog*. Children hold a pretend leash with hand outstretched; dog runs fast, between legs, slowly, in circles, jumps in air, chases a cat, goes to sleep.

Lesson #33: Partner Day

Objectives: To understand the importance of working together through various activities which foster positive interaction skills.

Materials Needed: Scoops* (1 per child; See App. 3)
Beanbags (1 per pair)
Balls (1 per pair)
A raw potato
A soft ball or stuffed animal

Class Outline:

A. Warm-ups* (See App. 1)
B. Activities
    1. *Scoops.* Pair children; give each child a scoop and each pair a beanbag. One partner tosses beanbag underhand to other, who catches it in scoop. Repeat.
    2. *Ball roll.* Change partners. Roll ball back and forth to each other. Roll ball while squatting, then standing. Toss ball or beanbag. Modify by decreasing size of ball and increasing distance between partners.
    3. *Races.* Change partners. Stand together with arms on each others' shoulders, while balancing beanbags on heads. Walk from one side of room to other. Next, balance beanbag on each foot and walk on heels across room.
    4. *Body Dance.* Change partners. As music plays, teacher calls out a body part. Partners dance with each other, touching that part of their body to their partner's. For example, thumb to thumb, knee to knee, elbow to elbow.
    5. *Pull and Pass** (See App. 2). Change partners. Lay head-to-head on ground on backs holding hands. One child holds beanbag between feet and lifts lower body up and over head, passing beanbag from feet to partner's feet. Continue passing.
    6. *Hot Potato.* Change partners. When music starts, children pass potato around circle. When music stops, person holding potato moves to middle of circle and game continues. When music stops, child in center moves back into circle and child holding potato moves into center. Continue.
    7. *Pass it on!* Children stand in a line. One child holds ball or animal under chin. Pass it to next child in line without using arms. This can be done with partners, in a circle, or as a relay where children pass the object, then run with it under chin.
    8. *Row Your Boat** (See App. 2). Children sit on floor, legs apart, facing partner. With feet touching, partners hold hands. One partner leans back and pulls the other gently forward, then pushes his partner back. Switch and repeat.
    9. *Nonlocomotion motion.* Change partners. Using a nonlocomotor movement, children interact with partner* (See App. 4).
    10. *Partner Sculpting.* Change partners. One is 'Sculptor,' the other is 'Clay.' Sculptor moves Clay in interesting position; Clay freezes. Switch and repeat.
    11. *Back to Back.* Children sit back to back with arms connected. Try to stand up simultaneously, pushing backs together. With backs together, lean side to side, forward and backward.

Lesson #34: Pirate Day

Objectives: To improve gross motor skills, balance, and coordination.

Materials Needed: A plastic pirate hook
A long 2x4 piece of wood
A blue sheet
A toy shark
Relay items (life jacket, plastic shovel, pretend anchor, lumme sticks)
Fake gold coins (1 per child)
Toilet paper tubes (1 per child)

Class Outline:

A. Warm-ups* (See App. 1)
B. Activities
1. *Overboard!* Children sit in a pretend boat (circle). Sing 'Row, row, row your boat'. The 'captain' (teacher) calls out a name and says, "Kelly, overboard!" That child jumps in middle and pretends to swim. Everyone else throws in a pretend line and reels them in. While pulling, say "1-2-3-4-5, (name) is still alive!" The child in middle takes seat. Repeat until everyone has had a turn.
2. *Captain Hook*. The teacher is Captain Hook, wearing a fake hook on one hand and kneeling in middle of the room. Captain Hook must stay on knees. Children are prisoners, trying to cross the bay. Captain Hook says, "Come little prisoners. I won't hurt you." The prisoners must 'swim' past Hook. If a prisoner passes Hook without being touched, he is safe. If he is touched, he becomes Hook. Repeat until all children have had a turn being Hook.
3. *Walk the Plank*. Use a 2x4 on floor. Children balance as they walk along the 'plank,' then jump off end, and pretend to swim to shore.
4. *Under the Sea*. Children hold edges of a large blue sheet. On the count of three, they lift sheet high and rush underneath, pulling sheet down behind them. Next, children hold edges of sheet and toss a toy shark on it.
5. *Pirate Relay*. Hop on one leg to life jacket, put it on, swim for shore, take it off, dig up a treasure, drag an anchor, row a boat, then run back. Modify relay to suit class.
6. *Coin Toss Walk*. Flip a Pirate's coin. If heads, everyone walks to left. If tails, everyone walks to right. Change directions from front to back. Use different locomotor movements. Then, give all children a coin and they toss and catch fake gold coins, or stand back and toss coins into a 'treasure chest' (box) lying on floor.
7. *I Spy*. Children use toilet paper tubes as telescopes to spy different things in room, such as items hidden by teacher, different colors or various shapes. Next, go on a treasure hunt. Give each child a specific "treasure" to hunt for.
8. *The Waves on the Sea*. (Sing to melody of "The Wheels on the Bus") 'The waves on the sea go up and down, up and down, up and down, the waves on the sea go up and down all day long.' Continue with: 'The shark in the sea goes snap snap snap;' 'The fish in the sea go swish swish swish;' 'The boats in the sea go toot toot toot.'

Lesson #35: Rocket Day

Objectives: To understand personal and general space while practicing locomotor skills and patterns.

Materials Needed: Aluminum foil
Toy rockets (or paper towel tube; 1 per child)
Plastic/paper plates (1 per child)
Balloons (1 per child)
Hula hoops (1 per child)

Class Outline:

A.   Warm-ups* (See App. 1)
B.   Activities

1. *I Am...* **THE SUN:** Children sit on bottoms with arms wrapped tightly around bent legs. Tuck heads down to knees. Lift feet off floor and balance on bottoms; hold position as long as possible. Let feet down and start again. **A STAR:** Children stand tall with legs wide apart and arms lifted out and above heads. Raise heels off ground and balance on toes; hold position as long as possible. Lower heels and do it again. **THE MOON:** Children lay on stomachs with heads lifted tall and legs bent up touching bottoms. Reach back and grab toes, then rock back and forth for as long as possible. Rest on stomachs for a minute, then repeat.

2. *Astronaut.* Children mold a large piece of aluminum foil to head for a helmet. Discuss gravity: on the moon, astronauts move in slow motion but on Earth, we can move as fast as we like. Use music that switches from slow to fast about every twenty seconds. Pretend to walk on moon, then back on Earth.

3. *Countdown.* Holding toy rockets vertically on floor, countdown from 10 to 1. After saying "one," everyone shouts "Blastoff!" and throws rocket in air. Repeat.

4. *Adventures in Space.* Teacher tells story while children pantomime* (See App. 3).

5. *Space Boots.* Each child uses two plastic plates as 'moon boots' to walk around room without lifting feet off plates.

6. *Space Buggy.* Use plate as steering wheel of space buggy. 'Drive' around room without bumping into each other. Drive on flat and bumpy moon surfaces.

7. *Bumping Asteroids.* Children pretend balloons are asteroids floating in space. Encourage them to work together to keep balloons in air and off ground.

8. *Flight of the Spaceship.* Children move in 'spaceship,' (hula hoop) not touching other spaceships. If their spaceships bump, both ships must 'land' (sit down) inside their spaceship with hands on knees. Spaceship takes off again when touched by Teacher.

9. *Musical Asteroids.* This is not a competitive game – no one gets OUT. Place several 'asteroids' (hula hoops) around room, one for every 1-2 children. As music plays, children walk around asteroids. When music stops, everyone must jump *on* an asteroid (inside a hoop); there should be more than one child in a hoop. Each time music stops, remove a hoop. Play until only one hoop is left. Children must work together to ensure that everyone gets in hoop when music stops.

Lesson # 36: Scarf Day

Objectives: To improve memory, listening skills and creativity.

Materials Needed: Scarves* (1 per child; See App. 3)
Kleenex (1 per child)
Hula Hoops (1 per child)

Class Outline:

A.   Warm-ups* (See App. 1)
B.   Activities
1. _Information Station_. Scarves are a very versatile tool for enhancing curriculum. They can be used as props or costumes. Through dance, they help express music and depict wind, waves, erupting volcanos, and other concepts. As props, large, colorful, lightweight scarves made from a translucent and flowing material offer endless possibilities for adventure in movement with drama and dance activities. Scarves can easily represent concepts such as fiery flames, air currents, tornadoes or billowy clouds. With a little imagination, scarves can be converted into instant costumes by wrapping and tucking them around the body for a cape, veil, skirt, diaper, gown or turban.
2. _I Can Fly!_ Give each child a scarf to use as wings. Hold two corners of scarf in each extended hand, with scarf behind them. Teacher say, "fly" and encourage them to stretch their arms way out and up.
3. _London Bridge_. Two people hold up scarf for the bridge while children walk under one at a time going the same direction. Bring the scarf down on "Lady" and catch a child under it. This child takes place of a bridge holder. Continue.
4. _Tissue Dance_. While music plays, children dance with a Kleenex. Encourage creativity. When music stops, freeze. Continue playing. Then, teacher calls out movements: circles, figure eights, angular movements, snake-like moves on floor, throw scarf in air, twist it, flatten it out on floor, drape it over head.
5. _Moving Scarves_. Each child selects a scarf and stands in middle of a hula hoop. Stay in spot and explore movements that can be done with scarves. Grasp ends of scarf and put under calf in order to lift leg without using leg muscles. Next, grasp scarf ends with right hand, as scarf cradles left forearm and wrist; lift without using arm muscles.
6. _Hoops_. Arrange hoops in a large circle. Children make following movements:
   - Standing in hoop, pass scarves to right while retrieving from left.
   - Stand outside hoop. Swish scarf back and forth from behind head to center of hoop on floor.
   - Stand with one foot outside and one foot inside hoop. Hook scarf between toes of outside foot, swing scarf in and out of hoop.
7. _Over Under_. Children stand in a line facing same direction. First child takes a scarf and passes over head to child behind. Second child takes scarf and passes under legs to child behind. Continue pattern.

Lesson #37: Sea Day

Objectives: To expand imaginations while learning to focus energy.

Materials Needed: Large blue sheet
Umbrella (optional)

Class Outline:

A.   Warm-ups* (See App. 1)
B.   Activities
1. *Under the Sea*.* (See App. 2) Demonstrate following motions: **Shark**: Lie flat on stomach. Hold hands above head with fingers pointing up for a fin. **Starfish**: Lie flat on back with arms and legs spread way out. **Jellyfish**: Lie on back with arms and feet up in air and wiggle them. **Eel**: Lie on side with straight-arms, hands clasped above head, straight-legs, toes touching together, and wiggle. **Turtle**: Curl body on ground, chest lowered to knees, forehead touching ground. Simulate ocean by waving sheet. Children use bodies to recreate ocean life under the sea (sheet). Call creatures in random order and varied speeds; children perform moves.
2. *Jellyfish Jiggle*. Discuss jellyfish using an umbrella as visual aid. Jellyfish have no bones; they are like a blob of jelly, shaped like an open umbrella. They swim by opening and closing their bodies, squeezing water from underneath, pushing them upwards. When they stop moving, they float down. Play slow music as children move like jellyfish. Open arms and push them down, floating on tiptoes. Then stop moving and fall to knees slowly.
3. *Octopus*. Teacher is the octopus and kneels in middle of room. Children are a school of fish and must swim to other side of ocean. Octopus says, "Come little fish; swim to the other side." Fish must swim past the octopus. Fish are 'safe' if they pass octopus without being touched. If touched, fish become octopus. Repeat.
4. *Rowing*. Children sit in a line on floor, legs apart, facing the same direction. Everyone makes rowing motions with arms at sides. Then everyone leans back at same time. Then children do the actions as teacher calls out the following: "Row," "Hit the deck," "Heads up," "Lean starboard (to right)!" and "Lean port (to left)!"
5. *A Walk With a Hermit Crab*. Teacher reads story as children pantomime movements* (See App. 3).
6. *Front of the Boat, Back of the Boat*. Say, "front of the boat" - children run to front of room. Say, "back of the boat" - children run to back of room. Randomly call out sea creatures from #1 (shark, starfish, jellyfish, eel, and turtle) as well as 'front of the boat' and 'back of the boat' and have them do the actions slowly and quickly.
7. *Message*. Children must correctly deliver a message from the back of boat to captain at front of boat Stand in straight line, facing back of room. Teacher is at back of line and taps last child; that child faces teacher, and watches teacher perform a simple series of hand movements. Only last person in line can see this, since rest of class is facing other way. That child taps next child in line, and passes movement on. Eventually, movement makes its way to front of line. Teacher shows class what original movement looked like...how much did it change?

Lesson #38: Shape Day

Objectives: To identify basic shapes by creating shapes with different body parts.

Materials Needed: Shape cards (laminated)
Beanbags (1 per child)
Ribbons (1 per child)
Elastic bands (sew 2 ends of 1 yard of elastic)

Class Outline:

A.   Warm-ups* (See App. 1)
B.   Activities

1. _Make a Shape_. Discuss how basic body shapes are small, tall, wide and twisted, but all kinds of shapes can be made emphasizing things or different body parts. Shapes can be made on floor, sitting, kneeling, standing or even in air. Challenge children to make shapes individually and as a group. After making shapes with bodies, use ribbons.
   - CIRCLE: Make a circle with arms, hands, fingers, moving circles with head and shoulders. Then everyone stand in a circle. Once in position, teacher says, "Wiggle only top half of your body. Now wiggle only bottom half of body."
   - TRIANGLE: Hop up and back and to the side to make a triangle.
   - RECTANGLE: Walk forward, slide right, walk back, and then slide left.
2. _Musical Shapes_. Place shapes randomly on floor. When music starts, walk, skip, or hop around shapes. When music stops, stand on a shape. Ask each child what color they are standing on. Other locomotor skills can be used as well as concepts of directions and pathways. "Can you walk backward in a straight line?" or "Gallop in a curved pathway around the shapes."
3. _Beanbag Toss_. Tape the shape cards to a wall at different levels. Children stand in a line 6 feet from wall. Give each child a beanbag. Teacher calls out a shape. Say "GO," and children throw underhand to the target. Then throw overhand.
4. _Shape Dancing_. Children dance to music. When music stops, hold up a card with a shape on it. Children look at card and quickly become shape on card.
5. _Ribbon Circles_. Give each child a ribbon. Make a circle on floor with ribbon. Stand in middle of circle. Stand outside circle. Put one hand in center, and then switch hands. Put one foot in center, then switch feet. Experiment with other body parts that can be put into center of circle.
6. _Mirror the Shape_. Pair children. While music plays, partners walk, run, or skip. When music stops, one child becomes a shape, and the other mirrors it. Reverse roles and repeat.
7. _Elastic Band Shapes_. Give each child an elastic band. Use hands and elbows to make a square with band; skip, walk, and jump while keeping band in square; make a triangle with two hands and one foot; hop, keeping band in triangle; make band into a circle on floor and stand in it, then skip around it; sit back to back with partner and put band between backs; create a triangle with partner at low and high levels using different body parts; as a group, form a triangle with band.

Lesson #39: Snow Day

Objectives: To increase coordination and body control, practice kinesthetic memory, and increase awareness of weight, shape, sound and gravity.

Materials Needed: Maypole with white ribbons* (See App. 3)
White crepe paper streamers
Yellow scarves (1 for every 2 children)
An ice cube

Class Outline:

A.   Warm-ups* (See App. 1)
B.   Activities
1. *Snow Angels & Ice Castles*. Children lie on backs. Pretend to be in snow and move arms up and down and legs open and closed several times; explain how this would make an angel in snow. Then get up and shake snow off by doing jumping jacks. Next, 'build' a solid ice castle of connected body shapes. One child stands in middle of room. Ask children one by one to 'attach' themselves to the group to form an ice castle shape.
2. *Snow Dances*. Children pretend to be drifts of snow swirling around a frozen object (Maypole). Give them basic directions (right, left, high, low). Then give each child a streamer for a free-form flowing dance. Play soft, slow music and encourage children to move streamers up, down and around in air.
3. *Snowflakes*. Discuss how it must feel to be a snowflake. Is it different from a raindrop? It's lighter, and not as wet. Do they fall the same way... make the same sound? Move your fingers like soft, feathery, delicate snowflakes. Stand and make a snowflake with whole body. Float up through space, then let gravity pull you back down. Whirl, twirl, and let the wind blow hard and gently.
4. *Snow Statues*. Work in pairs: One is the "Snow" and the other is the "Sculptor." ***Snow:*** Lie down on ground. Try to be soft and flexible like snow. When partner moves a body part, try to keep the rest of the body from moving. Relax the part that is being moved as much as possible to make it easy for partner to create a beautiful snow statue. Once positioned, freeze. ***Sculptor:*** Put on pretend gloves so hands will not freeze while working. Lift partner's arm and place it where desired. Pat snow carefully around arm to make it firm. Move partner's head. Position it, then pat it gently. Lift up from under partner's armpits to move body. How does the snow statue look? Now sculptor becomes the sun. Using yellow scarves, move arms slowly, making big round circles. Dance around snow statue, turning whole body. Keep moving and shining so the statue will melt. Melt one part at a time... first head, then let chin sink down to chest. Let each finger melt, then wrists, elbows, shoulders, knees, hips, ankles, toes. Now sculptor and statue switch places.
5. *Pass the Ice!* Children pass an ice cube around circle to music. When music stops, everyone claps for the one holding ice cube. Continue until ice is completely melted. Watch out for puddles! Children can jump over or into puddles when finished; it's great exercise!

Lesson #40: Stop & Go Day

Objectives: To establish a body control mechanism for stopping motion.

Materials Needed: Balloons
Butcher paper
Crayons (1 per child)
Hula hoops (1 per child)
Stuffed animals (1 per child)
A drum
'Stop & Go' Sign (sign with "Stop" on one side and "Go" on other)

Class Outline:

A.   Warm-ups* (See App. 1)
B.   Activities
   1. *Balloons*. While music plays, children keep balloons in air. When music stops, children grab balloon and freeze. Start music and repeat.
   2. *Draw the Music*. Use a large sheet of butcher paper to cover a table, and any music. Children walk around table with marker or crayon in hand, making movements on paper to the beat of music. Stop and start music at random intervals. Children color when music plays, and freeze when music stops. This activity combines art, music and movement.
   3. *Musical Hula Hoops*. This is not a competitive game – no one gets 'OUT.' Place several hula hoops around room, one for every 1-2 children. As music plays, children walk around hoops. When music stops, everyone must jump in a hoop; there should be more than one child in a hoop. Each time music stops, remove a hoop. Play until only one hoop is left. Children must work together to ensure that everyone gets in hoop when music stops.
   4. *Jump and Freeze*. Teacher beats a rhythm on a drum. Children jump while drum is beating, and freeze as quickly and as totally as possible. Teacher says, "Do not blink an eyelash, or make a sound!" Each child must have sufficient space. Repeat activity with varying rhythms or time lapses. Modification: explore different types of jumps: little/big, silly/serious. Freeze in different shapes: small/large, symmetrical/asymmetrical, rounded, pointed, low middle or high-level shapes, balance on one foot.
   5. *Animal Exchange*. Play any kind of music while children dance free-style with stuffed animal. Children develop body control as they learn to stop moving and freeze when music stops.
   6. *Red Light, Green Light*. Children line up at one end of room and teacher stands at other, turning sign back and forth.
   7. *Musical Hugs*. As upbeat, fun music plays, children dance around until teacher stops music. Children must find a partner to hug. Repeat; children LOVE this activity. Make sure all kids get hugged!
   8. *Electric You*. Pair children. Demonstrate cause and effect by having one child touch partner's shoulder; it moves. Touch knee, head, finger, elbow, and toe. Each part moves singularly.

Lesson #41: Teddy Bear Day

Objectives: To develop left and right recognition. To practice pantomime and improve listening skills.

Materials Needed: Teddy bears (ask children in advance to bring one; provide extras)
Masking tape
Beanbags (1 per child)
Bracelets (1 per child; or elastic bands)
Bubbles
A sheet

Class Outline:

A.   Warm-ups* (See App. 1)
B.   Activities
1. _Goin' on a Bear Hunt!_ Teacher reads story* (See App. 3) as children pantomime movements with their bears.
2. _Teddy Bear Freeze._ While music plays, children make bears dance the way the music makes them feel. When music stops, teacher yells "Freeze!" When everyone freezes, start music again and dance. Use different types of music to elicit different types of dancing.
3. _Beanbag Carry._ Create a path on floor with tape. Children follow path while balancing a beanbag on head, then on shoulder. Later use path to hop with beanbag on knee, then on foot.
4. _Left and Right._ Give each child a bracelet or elastic band. Encourage children to learn right and left. Move bracelet to different body parts, such as their right or left hand, arm, foot, leg, etc. Teacher says, "hold up right arm!" Children look at their reminder item and raise that arm. Continue with following ideas: shake right arm, hold left arm behind back, circle left arm, tap right hand on head, tap hands on hips.
5. _Bear Jump._ Explain that it might hurt the bear if they jump on it, so they must jump _over_ it. Children scatter bears around room. When music starts, jump over them.
6. _Bubbles._ Play music and blow bubbles for children to catch and pop.
7. _Bouncing Bears._ Toss bears on sheet. Raise and lower hands to make sheet move high and low.
8. _Hide and Seek._ Children go to corner of room and close eyes. Teacher hides bears all over room. When music starts, children find their bear. If they find someone else's bear, leave it and continue looking for their bear. Repeat.
9. _Bear Walk._ Put bear on back and do the bear walk: get on all fours and simultaneously lift right arm and leg, then left arm and leg.
10. _Goldilocks and the Three Bears._ Tell story of Goldilocks. Children act out story. Be animated and use different voices for characters. After reading the story, sort all bears according to size.
11. _Teddy Bear, Teddy Bear..._ Teacher reads rhyme* (See App. 3) as children pantomime movements with their bears.

Lesson #42: Tempo Day

Objectives: To acquire basic rhythm and tempo skills while improving attention span.

Materials Needed: Different styles of music (slow, waltz, salsa, jitterbug, rock, etc.)
Paper plates (2 per child)
Sticks (2 per child; dowel rods, maracas, etc.)

Class Outline:

A. Warm-ups* (See App. 1)
B. Activities
   1. *Sitting Down*. Clap out different rhythms with hands. Pound out different rhythms with fists. Pass out sticks and tap out different rhythms. Children watch as teacher taps out a sequence: tap sticks above head 3 times while standing, tap on floor like drums, turn around, tap knees and sit down. Add on or subtract depending on age of children.
   2. *Laying Down*. Children lay down on backs with feet and legs pulled up to chest in 'rock and roll' position. Rock to the rhythm of different styles of music.
   3. *Standing Up*. Children try following movements to learn rhythm: marching, walking, running, skipping, galloping, sliding, swaying, reaching, balancing. Play different kinds of music, or no music at all. They march quickly and slowly. Pass out plates. Children put one foot on each plate with barefeet and slide across floor as if ice-skating, first fast, then slowly.
   4. *Discuss words and phrases*. Fast, Slow, Moderate, Slow-to-Fast, Fast-to-Slow. Shake hands slowly, then fast. Wiggle fingers slowly, then fast. Pound the floor slowly, then fast. Rub hands together slowly, then fast.
   5. *Make a human machine*. One child comes to front and starts a movement, i.e., moving arms up and down while saying "Ba-Bing" over and over. Then add on. Another child attaches to first child making another movement and another sound simultaneously. Keep adding all children in a horizontal line. When all are attached, make the machine go faster by speeding up movements and sounds. Then slow it down by slowing movements and sounds. Raise up on toes and squat down to floor for different level changes.
   6. *Across the Floor*. Children say their name while making movements to match as they move across floor. For example, if child's name is Stephanie, repeat name quickly while running or hopping. Then slow it down, (Ssssssss-tepha-nnnnn-ie) and melt on floor or crawl. Say name choppily and zig-zag across floor. This is an activity that children of all ages love! They have so much fun hearing their names over and over again. Try marching, skipping, galloping and leaping across floor.
   7. *I'm a Bubble*. Children pretend to be a bubble while doing movements that have no particular rhythm: slow and light. Teacher says, "You are all bubbles. I will blow each of you into a big bubble. You will fill up with air and very slowly float to the other side of the room where you will burst." Then blow on the back of each child's neck as they expand their bodies.

Lesson #43: Train Day

Objectives: To strengthen stomach and back muscles and to establish parameters for personal space issues.

Materials Needed: Chairs (1 per child)
Train music (optional)
Toys (1 per child; put inside a box decorated to look like a train)
A sheet
A long narrow table
Number cards (make cards with numbers totaling number of children)
Masking tape

Class Outline:

A.   Warm-ups* (See App. 1)
B.   Activities: Rhythm
   1. _Down By the Station._ Children sit in chairs or on floor, one behind the other in a row. The person sitting in first chair is engineer. Teacher reads rhyme* (See App. 3). During first verse, coordinate arm motion with bicycling leg movement. During refrain, all pull imaginary cord for whistle, then hit imaginary bell in front of them. At end of refrain, first child runs to back of row and sits down as other children move one seat forward. Repeat until everyone has had a turn being engineer.
   2. _Trains & Stations._ Children stand in a line. As train music plays, children hold waist of person in front of them and shuffle feet along floor. When music stops, cool off engine by quietly blowing air out through mouth; lower shoulders and relax arms. Alternate starting and stopping music. Train can move backward. Then, sing "Choo-Choo the Big Train" and pantomime actions* (See App. 3).
   3. _I've Been Working on the Railroad._ Children do an obstacle course. Train travels up a hill, curves around mountain, over bumpy rocks, down slippery hill, through dark tunnel. Teacher says, "Oh no – the train fell off the tracks;" children fall to floor. Be aware of surroundings; don't trip over each other. Reverse sequence.
   4. _Add-on._ Each child chooses one action with accompanying sound. One by one, children hook onto each other, doing their individual movement.
   5. _Toy Train._ One by one, children choose a toy to act out. Child who guesses toy correctly pantomimes next. Ideas: bouncing ball, rag doll, snake, toy soldier, melting ice cream cone, jack-in-the-box. Freeze, speed up, slow down actions.
   6. _Tunnels._ Put a sheet over a table. Children kneel on hands and knees and hold ankles of child in front of them. 'Train' moves through tunnel.
   7. _Engine Number Game._ Each child pulls a number card from a container. When every child has a number, give them a minute to line up in the correct number order. If they do it correctly, they form a 'train' and circle the room. If they don't, they fall off the track. Children draw different numbers; repeat.
   8. _Train Wreck!_ Divide children in half. Each half forms a train and races across room. Then two trains hook up and follow a masking tape path. Children pretend to have a train wreck and everyone falls off the track.

Lesson #44: Travel Day

Objectives: To learn about countries of the world through kinesthetic intelligence.

Materials Needed: Passports (1 per child; fold white pages and staple along crease)
                              Tickets (1 per child; cards with seat numbers on them)
                              Chairs (1 per child)
                              American flag
                              Sombrero
                              Mexican Hat Dance Music
                              Igloo & Fans* (see App. 3)
                              Scarves (1 per child)
                              Several cotton balls
                              Chopsticks
                              Lumme sticks (1 per child)

Class Outline:

A.   Warm-ups* (See App. 1)
B.   Activities
    1. _My Passport._ Teacher says, "Let's go on a trip! Everyone must have a passport to leave the country!" Discuss what a passport is: a government document issued to a citizen for travel abroad. It certifies a person's identity and citizenship. Children 'travel' around room using different locomotor movements. Bring a real passport to show to class. Take a picture of each child and make everyone their own passport! Use stamps or stickers to put in passports.
    2. _Fasten Your Seatbelts._ 'Passengers' (children) board airplane with ticket in hand. Fasten seatbelts and get ready for take off. Children sway in chairs to music. Set up chairs in rows similar to an airplane; number chairs so children can find seats.
    3. _Here We Go!_ Locate and mark each country on map before doing activity.
       - **_Germany_**: Tell one of the fairy tales written by The Brothers Grimm and have children pantomime the actions: _Rapuntzel, Hansel and Gretel_ and _Rumpelstiltskin._
       - **_United States_**: Teach children the "National Anthem" and salute the flag! Then make a human flag: lay on floor for stripes, squat in ball for stars.
       - **_Mexico_**: Mexican Hat Dance. Children dance around sombrero.
       - **_Antarctica_**: Children dance in, out and around igloo like penguins with scarf tied around ankles.
       - **_Japan_**: Pick up cotton balls with chopsticks. Then do a Japanese Fan Dance.
       - **_Egypt_**: Children pretend they are camels – hunch backs with heads low. Make hump as high as possible. Then float down the Nile using Lummi sticks as oars.

Lesson #45: Zany Day

Objectives: To develop spatial relations concepts through activities which explore moving in and through different levels.

Materials Needed: Blindfold
Chair
Scarves (1 per child)
Noise-makers / Instruments (i.e., maracas, bells, shakers, etc.)
Hula hoops (1 per child)

Class Outline:

A.   Warm-ups* (See App. 1)
B.   Activities
1. *Who's Knocking?* One child sits in a chair, blindfolded. One by one, others come up behind and say "It's me!" with a disguised voice. Within 3 guess each, blindfolded child must guess who is behind them.
2. *Crazy Fruit!* Children sit in circle. Teacher assigns each child to be fruit. One child is 'It' and sits in middle. Teacher calls a switch command, for example: "apples change with oranges!" 'It' tries to steal a seat while fruits are changing. Child left standing is 'It.' Repeat.
3. *Use Your Toes.* Children use toes to pick up scarves and put them in a pile.
4. *Musical Story.* Teacher tells a familiar story. During story, children choose sounds to go along with it - the wind blowing, someone running, knocking etc. Give the children different instruments to make noise.
5. *In and Out.* Give each child a hula hoop to hide in. Teacher says "Jack-in-the-box," and children squat down in hoop. When teacher says, "Jack-out-of-the-box," children pop up. Mix sequence.
6. *Group Shapes.* Children scatter around room in random positions, some at high levels, some middle, some low. All are attached to someone else. Slowly, change level of position. Modification: divide children, and half watch as other half makes group shape. Change groups and repeat.
7. *Sending a Message.* Pair children and take turns. Write or draw a shape, name, or word on each other's back. Partner guesses what it is.
8. *Make a Space!* Divide children; half lay on floor, frozen in a shape. While music plays, other half runs around the children on floor, not touching them. When music stops, standing children freeze in position while making shapes with those on floor.
9. *Change Your Level.* Discuss different things that change levels, then act them out:
   - *Animals*: squirrels, birds, cats
   - *People in jobs*: mountain climbers, window washers, bridge builders, dancers
   - *Machines*: Cherry pickers, elevators, airplanes, light company trucks
10. *Kids on the Move!* Children line up at one end of room. Start walking at a low level, and rise slowly; when crossing middle of room, children should be on tip-toes with arms stretched high. Then slowly lower the level while continuing to walk. End at other side of room completely scrunched down to floor.

Appendix & Glossary

APPENDIX 1: Warm-Ups

Warm-ups provide a predictable routine at the beginning of each class for the children to follow. Warm-ups create a climate of emotional security and relax the class. Choose any of the following activities for warm-ups; each one should take from 3 - 5 minutes. If more time is available, consider doing ALL of the activities for warming up the children's muscles. Young children need to be encouraged to stretch from toes to fingertips to prevent injury.

1. **Drop and Pick Up**. Children drop and pick up different objects, depending on the theme of the day: a ball, feather, bean bag, or stuffed animal.

2. **Kneel and Rest Stretch**. Children kneel on floor with legs together. Rest bottom on legs, lower head to floor, and tuck hands to side on floor, pointing backward. Take two or three deep breaths and blow out. Relax and repeat.

3. **Rock and Roll Stretch**. Tuck legs into body, wrap arms around legs with feet off floor. Rock forward and backward, side to side.

4. **String Stretch**. Sit in pike position. Children pretend to tie a string to each big toe. Hold on to pretend string and pull it. As they 'pull' string, children pull knees and toes back towards the body. As they 'push' string, children push entire body forward with body laying on pike legs and toes pointing. Repeat pushing and pulling.

5. **Straddle Stretch**. Sit in straddle while pointing toes. Children pretend to throw a bag of candy in the middle of legs, then reach for the pretend candy. Say, "Put a pretend smiley face on your knees and make sure the smiley face is smiling up at the ceiling while you get the candy!" This ensures proper alignment and is a great stretch.

6. **Butterfly Stretch**. Sit in butterfly position* (See App. 2). Children 'fly' by flapping their 'wings' (knees). In position, touch nose to feet, move head side to side and in circles. Say, "What color butterfly are you?"

7. **Circle Stretch**. Children make circles with different body parts: head, arms, wrists, legs, ankles, hips, shoulders, knees and torso.

8. **Rainbow Stretch**. Stand with legs apart. Children reach high up to the ceiling. Sway arms over head from side to side, making a rainbow. Tree or flower stretch uses same movement, but tell children they are swaying in the wind.

APPENDIX 2: Photographs

Cendipede

Trapeze Artist: Low

Trapeze Artist: Medium

Trapeze Artist: High

Elephant

Hula skirt

Dinosaur

Lunge

Squat

Pike

Straddle

V-sit

Straight Body

Birdie-Perch

Butterfly

51

Soldier Jump

Tuck Jump

Crab Walk

Horsie Kick

Stink Bug Walk

Positive/Negative Space

Symmetrical

Asymmetrical

Pull and Pass

Rowing Boat

Shark

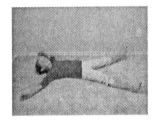

Starfish

Jellyfish

Eel

Turtle

52

APPENDIX 3: Lesson References

9: Cowboy Day   Make sheriff vests out of paper bags; cut up the center front of the bag then cut circles for armholes. Kids can tear a fringe along the bottom. Make a sheriff badge by wrapping a cardboard star with tin foil.

10: Dance Day   *Hula skirts*: make skirts from the comic section of a Sunday paper. Fringe one end of the paper three inches from the top. Fold other end a few times to form a waistband. Use large clips to secure two ends. Or, cut large rectangles from flowered material and have the children tie them around waists.
Shakers: toilet paper rolls with beans or rice inside. Tape up edges.

11: Dinosaur Day   "It's morning. You are lying on your stomach. The morning light warms the blood in your bony back plates. You begin to move – first a few twitches of the heavy tail, then lift your head for a look around. You stretch your back. The rest of the heard is starting to wake up. You stand up. Your little dinosaur babies are up, bumping into your sides as they stumble around. It is time for breakfast! Slowly, you move with your herd. You stop in the valley to munch leaves from the low bushes and ferns scattered around. You grind the green fibers with your flat teeth. Bite, chew, gulp, over and over. The little baby dinos are close by. One comes over for some free lunch. You drop a mouthful of chewed leaves and the little dinosaur snorts loudly as it eats. The day is getting hotter. You walk to the water. Cool liquid splashes down your throat when you raise your head high. Suddenly, you sniff a strange smell. Danger nearby! You turn and run through the bushes. The little babies are eater near a grove of palm trees. There is the danger! Allosaurus, the meat eater, is moving around the trees! Quickly, you push the babies toward the heard, snorting a danger call. The babies run back to the herd. You turn your back and swing your tail as Allosaurus comes around the trees. Wham! Allosaurus is thrown into a tree. He has a scratch on his side from your spike. You start running toward the herd, but Allosaurus is faster. He tries to bite you, but his teeth cannot bite into your bony plates on your body. The Allosaurus tries to move for your head, but you turn and swing your spiked tail. Wham! Allosaurus is thrown into a small ravine. You run and run. Finally, you are with the herd, gathered in a circle, stamping feet and twitching thorny tails. The baby dinosaurs are in the middle, snorting in fear. You join the defensive circle. But Allosaurus won't attack the whole herd. He is too afraid to fight everyone. He roars and stomps away. Slowly, you turn and begin to eat again. Bite, chew, gulp, over and over. When the sun begins to sink, you settle down on the rocky soil with the herd, your little babies by your side, and close your eyes to sleep."

12: Directionality Day   Direction cards: draw ↑ (an arrow pointing up) on 10 cards and ↓ (an arrow pointing down) on 10 cards.

14: Finger Play Day

Sticky Lollipops:
"Five sticky lollipops sitting on sticks,
Take a sticky lollipop and lick, lick, lick.

(They pretend to lick the stick then put one behind back)

Four sticky lollipops sitting on sticks,
Take a sticky lollipop and lick, lick, lick.

(Repeat actions with 3, 2, 1)

No sticky lollipops sitting on sticks!" *(They make frowny face and fold arms)*

Hands:
"Up and down, round and round   *(draw circle in air)*
Put your fingers in the ground   *(place fingers on ground)*
Over, Under,   *(hold hands high, then below legs)*

In between...   *(hold hands between legs)*
Now my fingers can't be seen!   *(keep hands between legs)*
Hands in front   *(hold hands out in front)*
Hands behind   *(hold hands behind back)*
Now my hands I can't find!   *(hands hidden behind back)*
Here's my left hand   *(shake left hand)*
Here's my right   *(shake right hand)*
Hands and fingers back in sight!"   *(wiggle fingers in front)*

Worms:
"Five little worms in the frying pan   *(wiggle all fingers)*
The grease got hot and
      then went BAM!   *(clap hands loudly)*
Four (3, 2, 1, 0) little worms in the
      frying pan"   *(wiggle all fingers)*
The grease got hot and it went BAM!"   *(clap!)*

Brown Bunny:
"Brown bunny, brown bunny,
Swish your furry tail. (Repeat)   *(Shake imaginary tails)*
Wrinkle up your cute little nose   *(Touch nose with finger and wiggle it)*

Put a carrot between your toes   *(Pretend to place carrot)*
Brown bunny, brown bunny,
Swish your furry tail. (Repeat)   *(Shake imaginary tails)*

Five Little Firefighters:

Five little firefighters	(Show five fingers)
Sleeping in a row.	(Rest cheeks on hands and close eyes)
Ring goes the bell,	(Everyone stand up)
Down the pole they go.	(Pretend to slide down pole)
They jump on the engine	(Pretend to jump onto a truck)
And put out the fire.	(Pretend to squirt with a hose)
Now they're back home--	(Sit down)
My, but they're tired.	(Stretch and yawn)

Clocks:

"Big clocks tick so slowly, tick, tock, tick, tock.
(pat hands slowly on legs while moving head side to side slowly)
Little clocks tick faster, tick, tock, tick, tock.
(pat hands a little faster on legs while moving head forwards and backwards)

Watches on your wrist go faster,
ticka-tocka-ticka-tocka-ticka-tocka-tick."
(pat hands fast on legs while moving head side to side fast!)

Children:

"Five little children went to school
(sitting down, move feet in front on floor, tapping up and down as if they were walking)
Five little children didn't follow the rules!
(shake head back and forth while shaking pointer finger side to side)
Five little children went jump, jump, jump...
(stand and jump three times)
One little kid went KERPLUNK!   (Fall down on floor)
Teacher called the mom and the momma said,
(hold hand to ear as imaginary phone)
No more children going jump, jump, jump!
(repeat with 4, 3, 2, 1, none)

Ten in the Bed:

"Ten in the bed and the little one said, Roll over. Roll over!
So they all rolled over and one fell off.
Nine kids in the bed and the little one said, Roll over..." Repeat.

Ten Little Indians:

"One little two little three little Indians,
Four little five little six little Indians,
Seven little eight little nine little Indians,
Ten little Indian (boys, girls, children, etc.).

16: Frog Day

Tadpole Story: "Curl up in a tiny ball. Now grow a tail. You're a tadpole! Swim around in the pond. Oh my! Feet are popping out! Now you can jump! Catch a fly with your tongue!"

17: Fun Day

Narrative: "Look at the funny way your arms are swinging. I like the way your head is bouncing around! And your legs – they are lifting forward and backward and sideways. Your back is bending and twisting. Your toes are jiggling! Oh, oh! Something is wrong! The string on your head just broke (drop your head - you can't move it any more). But your other strings are still pulling... your knees and elbows are lifting and your back is moving. Oh, oh! Now your arm strings are broken. Your head and arms can't move. But your back and legs are still bouncing. Your feet are jumping. Oh, oh! Now the string on your back is broken. Only your legs can move! They swing forward and backward while your feet dance. Oh, oh! Your strings on your legs are broken. Fall down to the floor while I walk around and look at everyone's broken strings. Let's give the tired marionette a minute to rest!"

19: Game Day

Chant
Group 1: "Here we come!"
Group 2: "Where ya' from?"
Group 1: "Africa!"
Group 2: "Whaddya' say?"
Group 1: "Come and play!"

20: Happy Day

Box Cube: Use a cereal box, shoe box, etc., taped together to form a cube. Wrap box in colored paper. Write the name of a favorite song or dance movement on each side of the cube.

22: Imitation Day

Story: "It's time for the cross-country race! We need a first place trophy to qualify for state finals! First, everyone **stretch**! Stretch out your arms. **Pull** them behind your head. **Twist and turn** your trunk to stretch out your back and stomach. Now **bend** over to loosen your leg muscles. Great, now **glide** to the starting line. Remember team: we need to **jump** out fast. Everyone stay together. **Squat** low. Concentrate. POW! We're off to the races. **Run** faster. **Dodge** the runners from the other team. **Kick** out from under them. **Poke** them with your elbows. Keep **running**, we're almost to the finish line. Do you see it? **Stamp, crawl, march, skip, drag, lunge, dive,** and **shake** to the finish line. Whatever it takes. Hooray! We made it! Now everyone **melts** to the ground in exhaustion. It's time for the awards. First place is OURS! We **jump** with excitement and **float** up to the front to accept the medals. We **wiggle** with pride when we realize we get to go to state finals!"

23: Indian Day   *Teepee:* Tie three poles together at top with rope, scarf, or rubber band. Spread three pole legs out at bottom. Toss a sheet over poles. Secure.

29: Nursery Rhyme
Day

Jack and Jill
  Jack and Jill went up the hill to fetch a pail of water.
  Jack fell down and broke his crown and Jill came tumbling after.
London Bridges
  London Bridges falling down, falling down, falling down.
  London Bridges falling down, my fair lady.
  Take a key and lock her up, lock her up, lock her up.
  Take a key and lock her up, my fair lady.
Ring Around the Rosey
  Ring around the rosey, pocket full of posey.
  Ashes, ashes, we all fall down!
Ride a Cock Horse
  Ride a cock horse to Banbury Cross,
  To see a fine lady ride on a white horse.
  With rings on her fingers and bells on her toes,
  She will make music wherever she goes!
Pussycat
  Pussycat, pussycat, where have you been?
  I've been to London to visit the queen.
  Pussycat, pussycat, what did you there?
  I frightened a little mouse under her chair.

Little Miss Muffet
  Little Miss Muffet sat on her tuffet, eating her curds and whey.
  Along came a spider, and sat down beside her,
  And frightened Miss Muffet away.
Humpty Dumpty
  Humpty Dumpty sat on a wall. Humpty Dumpty had a big fall.
  All the King's horses and all the King's men,
  Couldn't put Humpty together again.
Jack Be Nimble
  Jack be nimble, Jack be quick.   Jack jump over the candlestick!
Sing a Song of Sixpence
  Sing a song of sixpence, a pocket full of rye,
  Four and twenty blackbirds baked in a pie.
  When the pie was opened, the birds began to sing.
  Wasn't that a dainty dish to set before a king!
  The king was in his counting house, counting out his money.
  The queen was in the parlor, eating bread and honey.
  The maid was in the garden, hanging out the clothes,
  When down came a blackbird, and landed on her nose!

32: Pantomime Day   "It was late one night when I heard a big crash in my backyard. I got out of my bed and looked out the window. To my surprise, there, in my backyard was the weirdest looking creature I had ever seen. He must have been from Mars. The creature's body was egg-shaped and in the middle of it was a large star. Sticking out from each side of his body were three short skinny arms. Each arm had a hand. The hands were shaped like a piece of pizza. He had no legs, but he did have six feet shaped like the letter "X". Over his short neck was his head. It looked as if he were wearing a big paper sack over it. His ears were enormous, like Dumbo the elephant. His three eyes were shaped liked raindrops, and he was wearing glasses. Below his eyes was a tiny square-shaped nose. He wore a smile from ear to ear—just like a clown. Attached to the top of his head were two antennae. They were very curly. At the end of each antennae, were three fuzzy circles. Boy, was he a sight! I was relieved to find out that this creature was not from outer space, but from my dream!"

35: Rocket Day   "Get ready to blast off for a trip into space! It's time to get into our space suits. Step in with one leg and now the other leg. Put in one arm and now the other arm. Good job! Now that we're all suited up, let's step into the launch pad elevator and ride up to the spaceship. The doors are open. Now, step inside our spacecraft. Let's get ready to blast off. Fasten your seat belt, and hold on tight. All systems go! Minus ten and counting. Nine, eight, seven, six, five, four, three, two, one, LIFT OFF! We're in outer space! Let's get ready to leave our spacecraft and take a walk in space. Put on your air tank. Tighten your helmet. Make sure the lines are attached safely around your waist so you won't drift away. OK! Let's open the door. Get ready to jump into space. One, two, three, JUMP! Now that we're outside the spacecraft, we float around freely and slowly. It feels like we're swimming in a pool. Look out! There is a meteor shower! Move about quickly. Don't let them hit you! Keep dodging those meteors. Don't stop moving. Phew! It's over. Everyone stop moving. We're safe. Now, let's pull our safety line so we can return to our space shuttle. Pull with one hand and the other hand. Keep pulling. Good! Now, let's climb inside our spacecraft. We are safe. Now, take off your air tank and helmet and fasten your seat belt again. This is Houston Control. Prepare for re-entry. Let's prepare our space shuffle for re-entry. Get ready to start engines. On the count of three, push your starter button on the computer console: one, two, three. Good job! And now home we go - home to earth. Get ready for re-entry. Everybody hold tight as we break through the atmosphere. Well done! You're a great crew. Now hold on to that steering wheel as we begin our glide into the airport. Look! There's the airport. Hold on to that steering wheel and let's bring the space shuttle down nice and easy. We're almost home. TOUCHDOWN! Great landing! You sure are good pilots. And now we taxi to a stop. Let's open the door to the spaceship. Wow! What a surprise! Listen to that crowd and look at all those TV cameras. What a hero's welcome. Everyone wave to the crowd!

36: Scarf Day   Invest in some translucent fabrics of various colors. When making your own scarves, simply hem the cut edges. Most material comes in 47" or 52" widths. Use a scarf that is approximately 52" by 45" for group uses, such as making good wave effects, depicting a volcano, underwater scene, or clouds. For younger children, use a scarf approximately 36" by 47" for individual use.

37: Sea Day "Let's take a walk with hermit crab along the shore, by the sea and in the sand. Sit on the beach and rub your hands together when I say "scritch, scratch, scritch, scratch." Ready? Here we go. Hermit crab crawls out of the water (stretch arms forward in a crawling motion) and shakes the water off (shake head and arms) and begins to walk (rub hands together) scritch, scratch, scritch, scratch. He comes to a big, heavy rock and tries to move it (push with both hands), but it is too heavy (push harder). Look! There is a tin can. Crawl under it. (Children lean forward and scoop with both hands.) Look at that big, red bucket. Let's climb to the top of it. (Children reach high with hands.) It is too high. (Put hands down) Let's keep walking. (Rub hands together) Scritch, scratch, scritch, scratch. Stop! (Put hands down) See that little shell? (Point to the ground) Let's walk over to it. (Rub hands) Scritch, scratch, scritch, scratch. It looks just right for a hermit crab! But it is too small for us. Wave goodbye and let's hurry home. (Rub hands) Scritch, scratch, scritch, scratch, scritch, scratch, scritch, scratch. (Put hands down) Open the door (Reach out and pretend to turn a knob and open door) and come in. It's good to be home."

39: Snow Day   *Maypole:*   (Supplies needed)
¾" PVC plastic pipe cut to 6 ft. length
¾" PVC cap with 7/16" hole drilled in end (for ribbons to go through)
¼" flat washer (to thread ribbons through-goes inside cap)
¾" PVC threaded coupling
¾" threaded floor mount
18" long 2 x 12 for the base

Mount the threaded floor mount with four screws to center of 2 x 12. Screw threaded coupling into floor mount bracket. Slide PVC pipe into coupling. Thread ribbon through cap hole and washer. Tie ribbons on other side of washer with knot. Slide cap onto pipe with washer and knot inside. Spray paint pole and base if desired. Cut ribbons approximately 4-5 ft. long each.

41: Teddy Bear Day   *Goin' on a Bear Hunt*: (Children repeat each line after Teacher)
We're going on a bear hunt, we're gonna catch a big one, what a beautiful day!
We're not scared.
Oh, oh! Grass, long, wavy, grass.
We can't go over it, we can't go under it, we've gotta go throught it!
Swishy swashy, swishy swashy.

We're going on a bear hunt, we're gonna catch a big one, what a beautiful day!
We're not scared.
Oh, oh! Mud, thick, oozy mud.
We can't go over it, we can't go under it, we've gotta go throught it!
Squelch squelch, squelch squelch.

We're going on a bear hunt, we're gonna catch a big one, what a beautiful day!
We're not scared.
Oh, oh! A river, a deep, cold river.
We can't go over it, we can't go under it, we've gotta go throught it!
Splish splosh, splish splosh.

(Continue on next page)

We're going on a bear hunt, we're gonna catch a big one, what a beautiful day!
We're not scared.
Oh, oh! A forest, a big, dark forest.
We can't go over it, we can't go under it, we've gotta go throught it!
Stumble trip, stumble trip.

We're going on a bear hunt, we're gonna catch a big one, what a beautiful day!
We're not scared.
Oh, oh! A cave, a scary, dark cave.
We can't go over it, we can't go under it, we've gotta go throught it!
Tiptoe, tiptoe.

(Say the following verse all together and quickly)
OH NO – IT'S A BEAR!!!
Quick!
Through the cave, tiptoe, tiptoe,
Through the forest, stumble trip, stumble trip,
Through the river, splish splosh, splish splosh,
Through the mud, squelch squelch, squelch squelch,
Through the grass, swishy swashy, swishy swashy.
Run to the house, run up the stairs,
Oh oh forgot to shut the door!
Run back downstairs, shut the door,
Run back up, to the bedroom,
Jump into bed, pull up the covers,
WE ARE NEVER GOING ON A BEAR HUNT AGAIN!!

Teddy Bear, Teddy Bear
Teddy Bear, Teddy Bear, turn around,
Teddy Bear, Teddy Bear, touch the ground,
Teddy Bear, Teddy Bear, reach up high,
Teddy Bear, Teddy Bear, wink one eye,
Teddy Bear, Teddy Bear, slap your knees,
Teddy Bear, Teddy Bear, sit down please.

43: Train Day   ### Down By The Station
Down by the station, early in the morning.
See the little pufferbellies all in a row.
See the station master pull the little handle.
Puff, puff, toot, toot, off they go.
(Repeat song)

Choo-Choo
"Choo-Choo the big train is coming down the track now.
Stop (children extend hand in a stop-sign motion)
Look (put hand to forehead as if shading eyes)
And listen (put hand to ear)
Stop, look and listen (repeat actions).
Choo-Choo the big train is coming down the track now!"

44: Travel Day *Igloo:* Construct a large igloo by using empty plastic milk jugs and a hot glue gun. Be sure to cut off the necks of the jugs.

Japanese Folding Fans: Use a sheet of construction paper for each fan. Draw a design on both sides of the fans. Fold the papers. Fold the short end of the paper in approximately one inch. Turn the paper over and fold the same end one inch in the opposite direction. Keep folding back and forth until the paper has been folded completely. Tape one end of each paper. Spread out the folds to make a beautiful Japanese fan.

APPENDIX 4: Index Card Activities

Write each item on a separate index card. Put in a fun container; i.e., hat, basket, can, or brightly-colored bag. During holiday seasons, use specific paper and/or colors which cater to the appropriate holiday. For example, for Easter, hide activities in plastic eggs. For Christmas, write activities on green and red paper.

Hop on 1 leg
Everyone pop up like popcorn
Sing "ABC's" together
Stand up, turn around, sit down fast!
Pretend you're a bunny and hop around
Make an egg; roll over without cracking
Fly like airplanes!
Play faces: scrinch up (close eyes, tighten face) / open up (excitedly open eyes)!
Make a flower; all feet point in middle, then open up
Sing "Head, Shoulders, Knees and Toes!"
Sing "Twinkle Twinkle Little Star"
Make a choo-choo train
Be a butterfly
Make a shape with your body: girls make a circle - boys make a square
Be a ninja: Crawl, Climb, Run, Jump, Roll, Rescue!
Walk like a crab
Make a bridge with your body
Spell out the word "HAT" with your body
Swim in the ocean!
Walk backwards
Draw pretend circles in the air with hands, feet, fingers and elbows
Make snow angels on the floor
Hop in a circle
Balance on 1 leg

Action Cards

Wiggle	Stamp	Kick	Curl
Tap	Circle	Stretch	Walk
Run	Tip toe	Hop	Skip
Dance	Jiggle	Melt	Buzz
Roll	Crawl	Bend	Twist
Stretch	Push	Pull	Turn
Shake	Bounce	March	Kick
Spin	Pop	Lumber	Drag
Spring	Bolt	Hurdle	Trip

Locomotor Movements: any of the above movements which promotes a change of location.
Nonlocomotor Movements: any of the above movements which **do not** promote a change of location.

APPENDIX 5: Phrases to reinforce positive behavior

Incorporate these phrases into each class; it is important for children to hear positive feedback. As a teacher, you are responsible to be a role model and to help the children feel great about their creative movement experience. Add any additional comments which will foster a favorable learning environment.

* _Suggestion:_ *Children love to be recognized! At the end of a semester, have a ceremony presenting awards to the children for their hard work. Trophies or certificates are appropriate and fun for the kids!*

Wow, you are listening so carefully!
Look at all of the different ways your body can move!
Oh, you are SO creative.
I love your smile!
Look at the energy you are using to dance.
Great job! When I said FREEZE you stopped moving your body so quickly!
You are really using this entire room, that's great!
I like how everyone is moving in a different direction.
Thank you for listening so well and waiting to talk later.
I notice that you are trying so hard!
Sharing is Caring!
Look at how tall and straight you all are standing.
I can't believe how far you can stretch!
Look at (John) and how well he is balancing.
I am really enjoying you today.
Great job. You are all following the leader.
I can see that you are listening to me by the way you're body is moving.
Thank you for dancing with me today.
What was your favorite time in creative movement class today?
You get what you get, and you don't pitch a fit. *(Say when passing out props to children)*

Your Ideas:

. . . .

. . . .

. . . .

. . . .

. . . .

. . . .

APPENDIX 6: Parent Flyer Samples

Send monthly flyers home printed on bright, colorful paper with fun fonts and pictures. The first flyer should be a Welcome Letter introducing yourself and explaining the program. You may want to include how excited you are to teach the children! This ensures caretakers that the children are enjoying a valuable learning experience. Flyers should include suggestions for reinforcing skills at home, as well as the Objectives from the lesson outlines. Be certain that caretakers know that they can contact you at anytime by including the following sentence in each flyer: "If you have any questions or comments, please feel free to call me anytime at _____."

LETTER 1:

I would like to take the opportunity once again to tell you how much I enjoy your children. They are the highlight of my day, and I appreciate the trust you place in me!

Here are some of the fun activities we have been working on in Creative Movement Class:
1. *(List activities)*
2.

LETTER 2:

I want you to know how much fun I have with your children every day. They have all been working *SO HARD* in class and are so excited to show you what they have learned! Be sure to take an interest in and ask your child what they are learning each day.

Look at some of the skills we are learning this month in Creative Movement Class:
1. *(List activities)*
2.

LETTER 3:

I hope everyone had a great holiday! It's wonderful to be back. I hope your children are enjoying Creative Movement Class as much as I am. They are exceptionally FUN to teach! Here is the schedule for the next 3 months. Please ask your children what they are learning so they can show you! This helps them feel good about themselves and gets them excited to learn more!

January 10th: Animal Day. We will be studying...

January 17th: Cowboy Day. Have your child bring...

January 24th: Pirate Day. Prepare for an adventure on the high seas....

GLOSSARY OF TERMS

Aerobic – Physical conditioning designed to improve respiratory and circulatory functions which increase oxygen consumption. This is vital for children!

Agility – The ability to move with easily, quickly, and gracefully.

Alignment – The proper positioning of parts.

Asymmetrical Shapes – If a line is drawn vertically down the center of the body, both sides of the body are different.

Auditory Factors – The ability to perform an action by hearing the command and not seeing it.

Balance – When weight is equally divided while standing in different positions.

Charades – Game where a word is acted out by someone and others try to guess what they are.

Confidence – A feeling of belief in ones own ability to achieve and be successful.

Coordination – Harmonious functioning of parts for the most effective results.

Directionality – Which way you are moving: right, left, forwards, backwards, diagonally.

Dynamics – Variation and contrast in force or intensity in relation to movement.

Fine Motor Skills – Movements which promote and encourage the development of hand-eye coordination. Examples are turning and twisting hands and fingers.

Flex – Bending and stretching the muscles.

Flexibility – To move or tense a muscle by contractions.

Floating – To suspend, continually and slowly drifting.

Freeze – Not making any movements.

Galloping – A fast movement. Move one foot forward, and then move other foot to catch the first foot. Pretend to be a horse.

Gross Motor Skills – Movements of the large muscles of the body. Children who have well-developed gross motor skills tend to feel good about their body, and are self-assured when trying to master new challenges. Examples: running and jumping.

Hinges – Referring to joints. Permits motion in only one plane of the body. For example, elbows and knees.

Imagination – Having a creative ability. Being able to see things in your mind that are not really there.

Improvisation – To compose movement offhand or unrehearsed.

Isolate – Referring to body parts. For example, moving only the neck, or legs, or hips.

Kinesthetic – Sensory experience derived from touch.

Laterality – Relating to the side.

Leap – To jump with one leg stretched out in front from one place on the ground to the other.

Left – The part of your body where the heart is located.

Level – A horizontal line or surface in space. The body can move on low, medium or high levels.

Locomotion – The power of moving from space to space. Basic movements include: walk, run, leap, hop, jump, skip, gallop, and slide.

Lumme Sticks – ½" dowel rods cut into 10" pieces and painted bright colors.

March – To walk in a line similar to soldiers. Usually count 1,2,3,4, again and again.

Memory – The process of recalling what you have learned.

Midline – The median plane of the entire body or a specific part of the body.

Motion – A act or process of changing places.

Movement – To change or shift into another position.

Negative Space – Anywhere the body is not. For example, when making statues, negative space is the place where air can be seen.

Nonlocomotor – Repositioning the body without moving from space to space. Examples include to bend, twist, stretch, swing, push, pull, fall, melt, and sway.

Opposite – Across from, or the other side.

Pantomime – A story told by using body or facial movements.

Personal Space – The place which the body occupies. If you can touch anyone with your arms outstretched, they are in your 'personal space.'

Pike – Body position in which hips are bent, knees are straight, head is pressed forward, and hands touch toes or clasp knees.

Plie – (Pronounced, "plee-ay") A bending movement of the knees.

Point – Referring to the feet, to lengthen the muscles.

Positive Space – Anywhere your body is. For example, when making statues, your body is using positive space.

Punching – A quick movement. Extending hand and arm away from the body and then retracting it quickly.

Rhythm – An ordered recurrent alternation of strong and weak patterns in the flow of sound and movement.

Right – The part of your body opposite the heart.

Sequencing – The act of following directions in order. For example, give children three instructions verbally, and see if they can perform them in order.

Skip – A gait composed of alternating hops and steps.

Skitter – Forward movement across floor keeping feet parallel, never lifting feet.

Spatial Awareness – An understanding that the body is occupying space. Where you are in the room and what you are doing in relation to others.

Straddle – To stand, sit or walk with feet wide apart.

Symmetrical Shapes – If you drew a line vertically down center of body, both sides of body are exactly the same.

Tactile – Relating to the sense of touch.

Tempo – The rate of speed, or motion or activity.

Warm-ups – Exercises that flex and stretch the muscles so body won't become sore.

Acknowledgments

Edwin Arlington Robinson, distinguished American poet, once wrote of gratitude: "Two kinds of gratitude: the sudden kind we feel for what we take, the larger kind we feel for what we give."

For most of us, the first kind is the more familiar; that pleasure and warmth we feel when something is given to us. The second gratitude, while more rare, is more wonderful. How fine we feel when we have the opportunity to brighten the life of another.

- We feel deeply grateful for parents *extraordinaire* that gave us what we needed as toddlers, children and adolescents, and who continue to give tirelessly to us during our own parenting years.

    Thank you, Mom and Dad!

- We feel deeply grateful for siblings that have always been trusted confidants, strong allies and the truest of friends.

    Thank you, Sterling and Stephanie!

- We feel deeply grateful for husbands that are patient, supportive and loving, despite our long hours of teaching, typing and creating.

    Thank you, Michael, Daron and Gordon!

- We feel deeply grateful for children who love us no matter what, and always have a happy smile and warm hug for us.

    Thank you, Sterling, Savannah, and Stefan!
    Thank you, Stephen and Kassandra!
    Thank you, Jessica, Desiree, Cannon and Beaumont!

- We feel deeply grateful for the opportunity to give; to share our combined teaching experiences with other teachers and hopefully brighten the life of others.

    Thank YOU for buying our book; we hope it helps brighten YOUR life!

Teacher's Notes

Teacher's Notes

_____

_____

_____

_____

_____

_____

_____

_____

_____

_____

_____

_____

_____

_____

_____

_____

_____

_____

_____

_____

Teacher's Notes

Teacher's Notes

Teacher's Notes

_____

_____

_____

_____

_____

_____

_____

_____

_____

_____

_____

_____

_____

_____

_____

_____

_____

_____

_____

_____

Teacher's Notes

Teacher's Notes

_____

_____

_____

_____

_____

_____

_____

_____

_____

_____

_____

_____

_____

_____

_____

_____

_____

_____

_____

_____

_____

Teacher's Notes

_____

_____

_____

_____

_____

_____

_____

_____

_____

_____

_____

_____

_____

_____

_____

_____

_____

_____

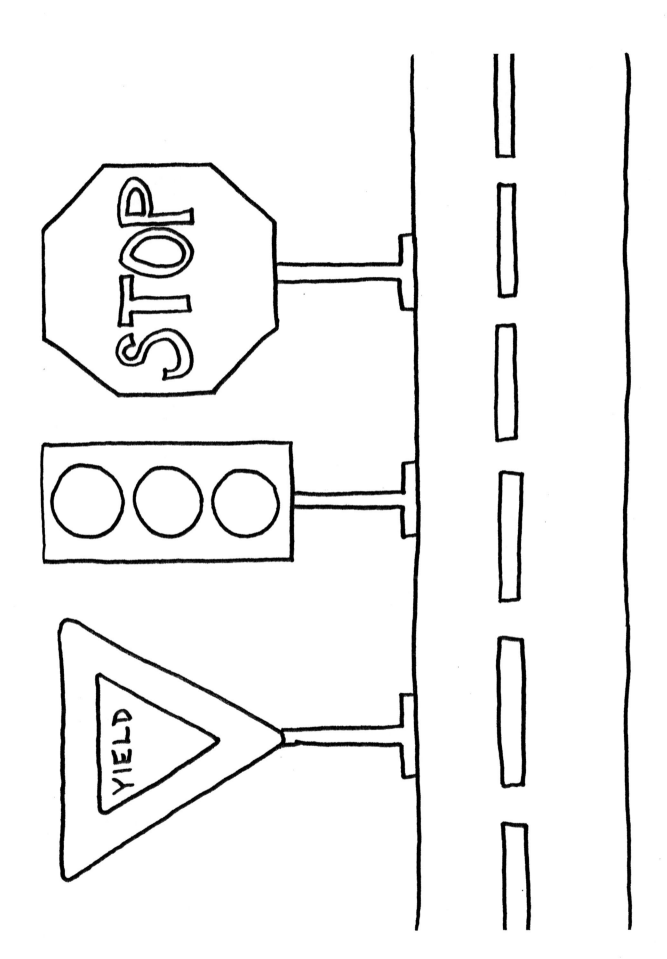

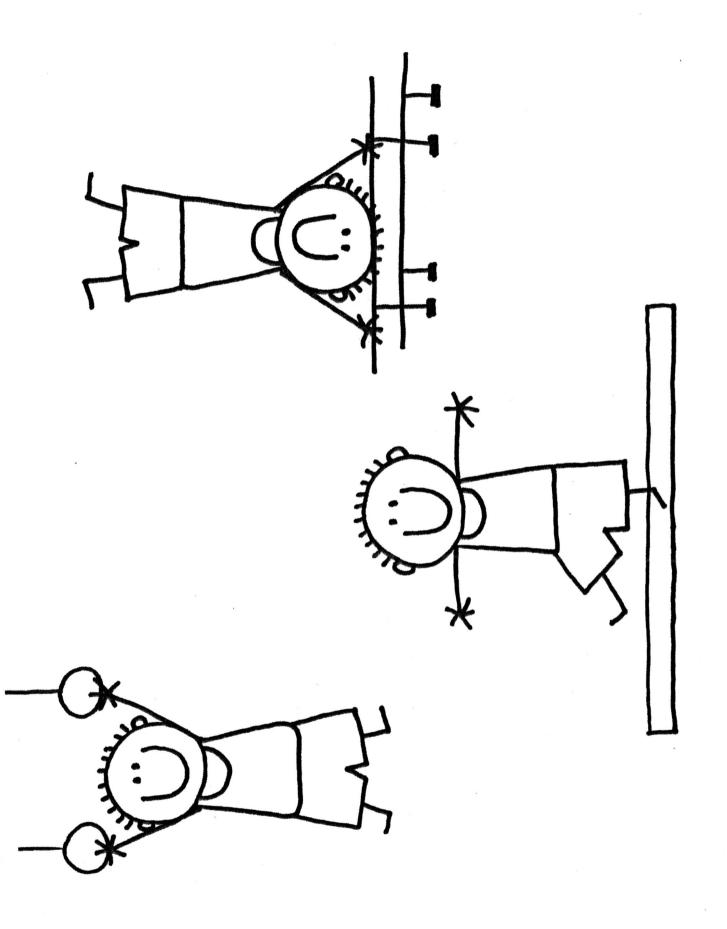

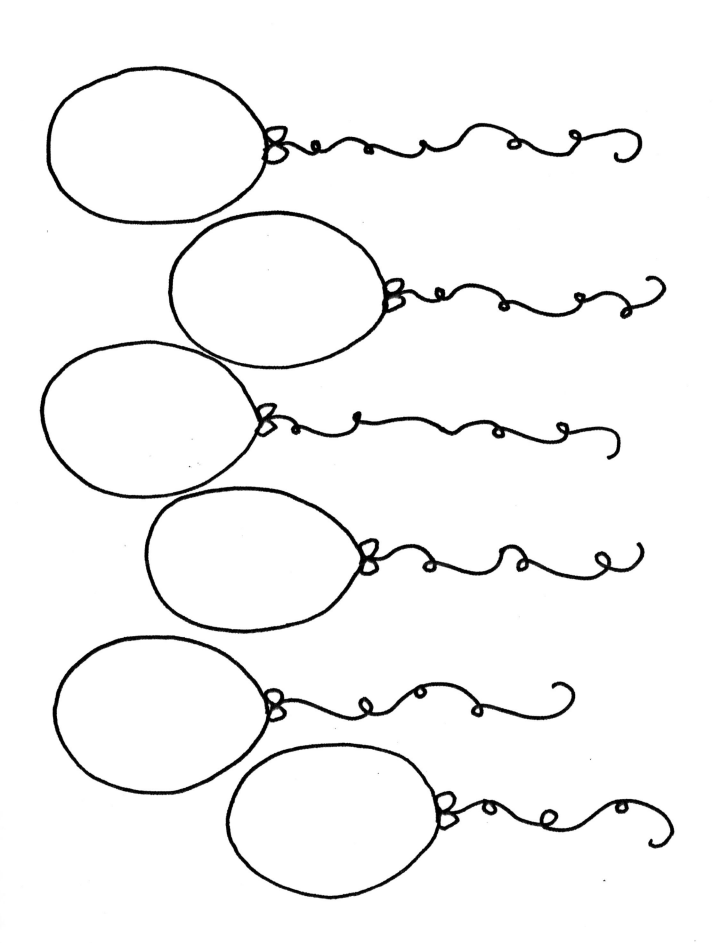

Printed in the United States
31343LVS00001B/3-48